BEAGLE TRAINING BASICS

The Care, Training and Hunting of the Beagle

y Bill Bennett

Doral Publishing, Inc.
Wilsonville, Oregon
1995

Published by Doral Publishing
8560 SW Salish Lane #300, Wilsonville OR 97070-9612.
Order through Login Publishers Consortium, Chicago IL

Copyedited by Luana Luther.
Cover design by Mary Jung.

Second Printing, 1996
Printed in Canada

Library of Congress Card Number: 94-74083
ISBN: 0-944875-33-5.

Bennett, Bill, 1941-
  Beagle training basics : the care, training
and hunting of the beagle / by Bill Bennett.
-- Wilsonville, Or. : Doral Pub., 1995.

    p. : ill. ; cm.

  Includes bibliographical references and index.

    1. Beagles (Dogs) 2. Beagles (Dogs)--
Training. 3. Hunting dogs--Training.   I.
Title.

  SF429.B3B   636.753 dc20

To Joseph F. Chambers, Col., USAF, (Ret.)
The man who showed me the way.

Acknowledgements

The writing of this book has heightened my awareness of the vast number of friends, colleagues, and family members who have contributed to its successful completion.

Deep graditude goes to my wife, Hanna, whose encouragement, patience, and confidence in me is absolutely astonishing; to my son Carl, who without complaint, performed an endless list of tasks necessary to finish the job; and to my entire family for their interest and support.

Acknowledgement is due to Dr. Kevin Reed, DVM. of Jonesboro, Arkansas, who provided valuable technical information for the manuscript.

Deep appreciation goes to the H & T Staff and my fellow employees of the Jonesboro Human Development Center, Jonesboro, Arkansas and my fellow Volunteer Hunter Education Instructors of the Arkansas Game and Fish Commission.

A special thanks is due to my friend, hunting partner and colleague, Robert Clay and to Roger Brand, Walnut Ridge Arkansas who provided some of the photographs.

A special acknowledgement is due to Alvin Grossman, publisher of Doral Publishing, Inc., whose knowledge, patience and guidance have been a godsend, the entire staff of Doral Publishing, and Joan Bailey, whose advice and counsel were greatly appreciated.

Contents

Introduction

The prospect of selecting, training, caring for and developing a puppy into a finished hunting dog can overwhelm anyone who has never undertaken the endeavor. The fear of making critical mistakes or becoming discouraged can spell failure for the beginner.

Self-confidence and knowledge are the key ingredients needed to accomplish the task. The problem is finding the knowledge to learn the process. One option is to find an experienced trainer with sufficient time available to coach the beginner through the step-by-step process. Unfortunately, although some of these experts exist, they are extremely rare.

Another option is to obtain the knowledge from a written source, such as a book. Unfortunately, specific literature on the care, training and hunting the beagle is sparse and fragmented at best. Current material on the little hound is limited to show and field-trial activities. Gun-dog writers of national outdoor sports magazines occasionally attempt to bridge the gap, but the scope of these articles is usually limited.

This guide is written primarily for the beginning or novice trainer who has never prepared a Beagle for rabbit hunting. However, it will also be valuable to the more experienced owner-trainer. It guides the reader through puppy selection, kennel facilities, general health care, self disciplines of training, yard training, the stages of field training, and the addition of a second dog. It is a step-by-step process that has proven effective for a number of Beagle owners. It will provide the necessary knowledge and self confidence for the beginning trainer to complete the task successfully. When followed, it will lead to quality time in the field with the hunting Beagle.

Photo courtesy of Anderson's Big Creek Kennels.

Rabbit Hunter: Traditional - Simple - Complicated

Weathered face. Scratches on hands and arms. Eyes of deep concentration. Old, yet young and inquisitive.

Tattered old hunting clothes. Snags from briars and thorns. A trusted shotgun. Old, yet serviceable. Gauge inconsequential. Ten-inch rubber boots. Worn laces. Draped over shoulder a "possibles" bag containing emergency items. Extra gloves, dog leash, a length of rope. Vest full of shells. Worn from much use, not unlike the man himself. Blaze-orange vest with matching cap. Bill protruding to block out the sun. Overalls, heavy, warm. Legs showing wear from briars and brush scars of many hunts.

A loner, yet friendly. Fiercely independent. Admired by many, especially his own kind. To others, a fool, immature, insane or at least adolescence delayed. A hunter but not just any hunter. He is a rabbit hunter. He braves early-morning frost, cold, subfreezing temperatures and raw wind, in pursuit of his quarry.

He is a lover and admirer of dogs. Not just any dog, but Beagle dogs. His heart leaps to the strike of a hound on a first-found scentline. And it pounds at the full cry of his hounds as they methodically circle the elusive target in a long, looping circle. He knows his Beagles by each unique tongue. He moves a few steps in the direction of their clamoring excitement, reassuring himself they will not go out of hearing. For to him, listening to the dogs work, assuring himself they are in no danger, is the hunt. He endures the long silent checks with everlasting impatience, assured that the dogs will find the line and turn the quarry in his direction. He is confident that the race will come full circle. He will see the quarry. He might shoot. He might not, allowing it to pass, providing an opportunity to listen to the dogs a while longer. For he knows that individually and collectively they too enjoy the game.

He is a conservationist. He takes only what he can use. He has learned to appreciate the total outdoor experience in its unique setting. He appreciates the rise of a covey of quail, the honk of the geese, the melody of the song bird, the call of a circling hawk, the flaming autumn colors and the drab brush and brambles that make up his wilderness.

He is tolerant of fellow hunters of duck, deer, coon and squirrel. He will indulge in some of these activities on occasion. But his domain is the swamp, the cotton patch, the ditch bank, thicket, fencerow, honeysuckle and canebrake. To him, this is wilderness, the home of the cottontail and swamp rabbit. He knows that wilderness, much like beauty, is in the eye of the beholder.

More often than not, he is solitary. This may belie his profession. But in his mind, he is not alone. For he has his dogs. They understand him and accept him, as he understands them. As they follow their instincts to hunt, he is bound with them and to them as other men through the centuries have been bound to their own instincts to hunt. To search. To explore. To see. The bond is buried in his psyche. He and his dogs rehearse the drama much the same way as their ancestors, an interplay neither completely understands. For to a rabbit hunter, there is no urgent need to understand. There is only the urgent need to be out there.

Rabbit Hunter: Traditional. Simple. Yet complicated.

A Look at the Beagle

A History of the Beagle

The origin of the Beagle cannot be determined with certainty. Early records are both speculative and inadequate, leaving the breed's true beginnings unknown. Yet, as far back as 400 years before the birth of Christ, ancient records show that the Greeks used scenting hounds for sport. Those popular sporting events were adopted by the Romans, who continued the tradition.

Further, there is general agreement among historians that in 600 A.D. King Arthur and his Knights of the Round Table owned white scenting hounds of excellent quality. The debate continues among experts whether the earliest breeds were scenting hounds used to develop the current gun-dog breeds or vice versa. Nevertheless, the ancient scenting hounds were the ancestors of the current scent-trailing Beagle hounds of today.

In the year 1027, William the Conqueror of Normandy invaded England and Wales. It is believed he was accompanied by two distinct hound breeds. One was the "sight chase" hound similar to the Greyhound. The other was a scent-trailing hound much like the Bloodhound. Both of these breeds became popular sporting dogs in the British Isles.

By 1066 in England, every respectable nobleman and gentleman kept a pack of hounds and used them to hunt a variety of game, including pheasants, squirrels, rabbits, hares and deer. Contrary to popular belief, the fox was not necessarily the game of choice for hundreds of years.

In the 1400s, hound owners began to divide their packs by size, using larger "buck" hounds to chase deer and the smaller hounds to chase a variety of smaller game. These smaller hounds were called "Begles" — with no "a" in the name.

The Beagle's ancestors were scenting hounds of ancient Greece and Rome. Photo courtesy of Anderson's Big Creek Kennels, Jonesboro AR.

The word Beagle is derived from a combination of French and old and middle English, with the root from a Latin word meaning gullet. Modern-day enthusiasts simply refer to the Beagle as the "little hound."

During the following 400 years, hound owners conducted considerable breeding experimentation. The goal of these pioneer pack owners was to reduce the size of the tall, rangy hounds of their day. The result was the Miniature Beagle or Little Harrier only five inches high. This small breed was considered a novelty in its time. It could be carried in a man's pocket or in a small wicker basket affixed to either side of a horse's saddle.

Fortunately, owners quickly discovered that this miniature breed was less than adequate for hunting, and the breeding trend was reversed to increase size and stamina. By the early 1600s, the versatile, smaller hound was the breed of choice for rabbits and hares. In the early 1700s, two distinct groups of hounds were again popular—the "buck" hound, similar to the breed of the 1400s, and smaller "hare dogs" or Harriers.

By the 1800s, fox hunting became the game sport of choice, establishing the larger breed as the "Fox Hound." The smaller breed was divided into two separate hare hounds, the Southern Hound and the North Country Hound. These smaller breeds exhibited startling contrasts. The Southern Hound was slow, ponderous, long-eared and deep-voiced. The North Country Hound was fast, nimble and tireless in pursuing game. The northern version also possessed a high-pitched, chopped mouth.

In the middle 1800s, the Rev. Phillip Honeywood of Essex, England, established a pack of hounds from which the modern Beagle was established. The Honeywood pack was derived from the blood lines of the Otter Hound and the Bloodhound. Honeywood and his companions became known throughout England as the "Merry Beaglers of the Meadows," and the sport of chasing hares and rabbits escalated in popularity, not only in England but in France, Italy, Greece and other parts of Europe.

In the United States, the earliest record of rabbit hunting with hounds was documented in 1642 at Ipswich, Massachusetts. Prior to the Civil War, hound hunting for deer and rabbits had become an established tradition. The majority of the hounds resembled straight-legged Bassets or oversized Dachshunds. Their coloring was predominantly white with splotches of black or tan.

In the 1870s, General Richard Rowlett of Carlinsville, Illinois, imported Beagles from England and developed the current strain of

The Beagle was founded from a pack of English Beagles. Photo courtesy of Anderson's Big Creek Kennels.

American Beagles. Unfortunately, records do not identify the specific packs of English Beagles from which he obtained his breeding stock. Nevertheless, Rowlett's importation served as the turning point in American Beagling. The Rowlett strain, also known as the Kerry Beagle, brought handsome lines and beauty to the little scent hounds, heretofore unknown in hunting. These Beagles proved to be tough, vigorous and tireless. Except for their smaller size, they resembled The Saddle Back and Walker Fox Hounds.

James Kernochan and a Mr. Arnold of Providence, Rhode Island, followed Rowlett's lead and also imported Beagles from England. Arnold imported his pack from the famous Royal Rock Beagle Pack in 1896. Kernochan and Arnold influenced the development of the current American Beagle by establishing field trials in the late 1800s.

The National Beagle Club was founded in 1888. Field trials spread rapidly through the United States carrying designated points for championship status. Generally, the hounds were divided into two

The handsome lines and beauty come from the Kerry Beagle strain. Photo courtesy of Anderson's Big Creek Kennels.

A Beagle can be any hound color. Photo courtesy of Anderson's Big Creek Kennels.

The Beagle is excellent with children. Photo courtesy of Tina Bennett Kornblith, Glen Ellyn IL.

A Beagle, a child and snow. What better combination.

Beagles enjoying a day in the fields with young friends.

The leash offers an opportunity to be close.

classes according to height, 13 inches and under for one class and 13-to-15 inches for the other class. These two height classes continue to serve as one of the current field- trial standards. In England, the maximum height standard is 16 inches.

The cottontail rabbit is the most popular game animal for modern field trials in the United States. However, alternatives are available, depending upon locale. In some southern states, the larger swamp rabbit is a challenging quarry and is popular among Beaglers even though it does not rank high on the list for field trials. In the northern sections of the nation, field trials are conducted on the elusive snowshoe rabbit or varying hare. The northern trials are a tradition credited to the Northern Hare Beagle Club of North Creek, New York. The club began these trials in 1916.

While the Beagle's specific origins may be shrouded in long-lost ancient records, its heredity is steeped in a proud, colorful history and tradition, making the Beagle one of the oldest breeds on the American scene.

The Beagle Personality

The Beagle is often called the "Big-Little Hound" by those who know the breed. But to the uninformed, the designation can be misconstrued or misunderstood. To the casual observer, the Beagle is simply a hound—stubborn, obstinate, and hard-headed with few if any redeeming personality traits. But hidden beneath the Beagle's exterior lies a warm, endearing personality that has given him special status and sets him apart from the other hound breeds. In addition, the unique Beagle personality allows him to serve multiple roles.

The Beagle is in fact a true hound, descending from scenting hounds originating in ancient Greece before the Christian Era. The breed's ancestry has provided the dog a marvelous sense of smell and a streak of stubborn determination—traits that are unique to the family of scenting hounds.

The Beagle is a strikingly handsome dog, a miniature mirror image of the larger Foxhound or Harrier breeds. The Beagle's feet appear overly large for his small body. He possesses a handsomely shaped head with wide nostrils, black nose and squared muzzle, which is flagged with long, thin ears extending below his lower jaws. His expressive eyes sparkle with a glint of playfulness. His tail is strong and tapered. It is

The Beagle can be an excellent hunting companion and a beloved family pet.

carried erect but not excessively forward. In a sense, it reflects an air of pride and dignity. His front legs are strong and straight. They parallel his powerful hind legs, which provide a clue to his toughness. This 13-to-15 inch compact package comes wrapped in a short-haired, dense, tough, waterproof coat, which differs in color from the popular traditional tri-colors of white, tan and black to almost completely white.

The Beagle is an intelligent dog who adapts easily to man's domain with proper training. He is content living enclosed in a pen in a suburban backyard or in an apartment in a high-rise building of a major city. He is perfectly comfortable serving as a companion to a lonely single person or to a family with a group of active children. Being non-aggressive. the Beagle is an excellent choice as a child's pet, providing

Hunting rabbits is a family sport.

Points lead to championship status. Photo courtesy of Anderson's Big Creek Kennels.

Health standards are rigidly enforced at field trials. Photo courtesy of
Anderson's Big Creek Kennels.

that appropriate discipline is maintained for both species. The age-old
parental fear of dogbite is almost non-existent due to the Beagle's
childlike charm and nature.

A Beagle is easy to keep, likes people, is willing to please and is a
most pleasant pet by all standards despite an occasional display of
stubbornness, which he is unable to control. His small size and
outgoing nature contribute to his immense popularity. In 1987, the
American Kennel Club registered an average of 50,000 individual
Beagles per week, and the breed's numbers continue to grow unabated.
These numbers show that the Beagle's occasional lapse into hound
stubbornness is far outweighed by the dog's many favorable qualities.

There are certainly those individual Beagles whose genetics render
them extremely temperamental and reluctant. But even these "hard-

core" hounds can become outstanding pets and hunters with proper handling and training. Beneath his outward appearance, ignoring commands on the pretense he is mostly deaf, he will eventually respond to his owner with affection and loyalty. Persistence, patience and consistency are the keys to winning him over.

The Beagle's boundless energy and stamina demand that he be exercised regularly, whether housed indoors or in a backyard pen. The dog is amazingly strong for his size. After proper leash training, he handles easily and will show his delight to be with you every time he sees the leash. He has the intelligence to learn that the leash means an opportunity to be with you.

An ability to relate to people in a positive manner allows the Beagle the opportunity to fill the dual role of family pet and weekend hunting companion. There are those who argue that the pet Beagle is a spoiled

The Beagle's work ethic will bring pride to any owner. Photo courtesy of Anderson's Big Creek Kennels.

dog, lacking toughness and staying power on the scent line. But numerous owners have proved this contention wrong. The key to developing this dual-purpose Beagle is maintaining the proper routines, providing the dog a chance to learn how to work scent lines as well as the proper discipline and training. A word of caution at this point: Hunting activities should be limited until the dog is conditioned properly to withstand the rigors of the hunt.

The endearing nature of the "Big-Little Hound" is perfectly suited for the dual role of pet and hunter. He is excellent with children, and in time the entire family can enjoy hunts together.

The Beagle's instinct to sniff, investigate and trail borders on the phenomenal. These inherited hunting traits are his rightful throne in the canine world. His ability to stay with a scent line and trail until the quarry is intercepted is, after all, his destiny. His toughness and compact size allow him to operate with amazing efficiency in all types of terrain that harbor rabbits. His stamina and strength are truly awesome in the field. His loud, bawling howls are the purest form of music to the rabbit-hunting Beagle owner.

The non-aggressive personality suits the Beagle perfectly to the family sport of field trialing. In these events, the little hound is placed with dogs of like size and age. At times, trials pair two dogs in a "brace" for a race. Other events require the hound to be placed with a pack. Judges award points for hunting ability and overall performance. Through a series of trial events, the accumulated points awarded to a dog can lead to championship status. Most of the field trials hold special showings for "bench championships." The judges at these events focus of appearance and conformation.

If you love Beagles, enjoy competition in a family-oriented environment and like to meet other Beagle owners, field trial events would be an excellent sport. For the true Beagle enthusiast, just listening to the music of the hounds bawling and howling on a hot scent line is reason enough to attend.

It is important to keep in mind, however, that the Beagle trial sport places the primary focus on hunting ability by comparison to the other dogs in the pack. The quarry is not bagged. Entry to those events requires that the dog meet certain health standards and be registered with a recognized sponsoring organization. Some of these organizations include the American Beagle Club, the National Beagle Club and the American Rabbit Hound Association. For more information, contact one of these organizations. (Addresses are contained in the appendix.)

In addition to the Beagle's charming nature, enthusiastic demeanor and willingness to please, he possesses a work ethic that always justifies pride in ownership. He excels as a winner in the show ring, a narcotics investigator for the United States Navy, and is a tireless worker at almost any assignment. He is a weekend companion to millions of hunters pursuing white-tail deer in the Northern United States and Canada, chasing rabbits across the farmlands of America, following the elusive snowshoe hare in the Northern United States and Canada, and flushing and retrieving pheasants for English noblemen. He serves patiently as a family pet, follows at the heels of a country boy to his favorite haunts and serves as companion to the lonely. He performs all of these duties without a single complaint.

In return, the Beagle expects only an affectionate pat, good care and an appreciative owner. He is always ready to respond with a lifted paw, a soft lick across the hand, a wet lick on the face and a soft nuzzle against the leg of the owner, whose faults the dog either ignores or forgets. The Beagle is a soft, warm marshmallow encrusted with a cast of steel—and all of him totally lovable.

Field trials are great family sport. A group of proud winners.
Photo courtesy of Anderson's Big Creek Kennels.

Chapter 1
PUPPY SELECTION

Why a Beagle? Given the opportunity and training, won't most dogs hunt rabbits? Probably so, but Beagles and rabbit hunting were just made for each other. The typical Beagle is a tough little dog. His size, however, is no measure of his heart. He is well known for his intense stubbornness, which is a primary hunting trait. Once on a scent line he will continue to trail until the rabbit is bagged, goes down a hole, or either the dog or the rabbit is intercepted.

Why select a puppy rather than an older dog? You are looking for a companion that you can train and can hunt with you. Unfortunately, dogs more than 12 to 16 weeks old begin to develop some undesirable habits, such as excessive barking, jumping on people, ignoring verbal commands and generally unruliness. Certainly, most Beagles can be trained to hunt, given the proper time and effort. But the older the dog, the more training problems will be encountered. Thus, there will be more frustration on the trainer's part. If you are skilled and experienced in dealing with these problems and enjoy the challenge of curing extra behavior problems, so be it. For the novice owner-trainer, it is strongly recommended that the goal be a puppy between eight and 12 weeks of age. Both pup and owner can bond and grow together through the training process.

The Beagle's durability and stamina are no less than astonishing. He will take on any terrain, be it rocky hill, briar patch, honeysuckle thicket, weed-covered field, swamp or canebreak. He is capable, with appropriate training and conditioning, to perform all day long in all kinds of weather. He lives to hunt. While his nature is generally affectionate and endearing, he is remarkably durable.

It is sad indeed to see a novice owner buy a young Beagle that will never attain his potential as a trained hunting dog. Likewise, it is sad to see an enthusiastic novice hunter-trainer with all the best intentions fail in his efforts to train his young dog because of insufficient knowledge and confidence. His dog never achieves his potential as a useful hunting companion. That is one reason why the puppy-selection process is so important. The following points have served over the years and if used correctly should help guide you to choosing the very best puppy possible.

Selection is one of the most important aspects of Beagling. Remember, this puppy will be a long-term companion. He will become a very important part of your life. So how do you know what to look for in selection? You will want to decide in advance whether you prefer a male or female. It has been my experience that the female is usually a little sharper in training, but for other reasons you may want to select a male. Regarding hunting ability, the male-female issue is rather moot following training. It boils down to a matter of personal preference. The primary goal is to select a puppy who possesses good hunting bloodlines, who exhibits a pleasant personality, and who displays the natural instinct to hunt.

Is a registered pedigree a primary consideration? For many owners anything less than an outstanding pedigree is beyond consideration. If

What does the appearance of the dogs tell you? Satisfied?
Photo courtesy of Anderson's Big Creek Kennels, Jonesboro AR.

you plan to become involved in the breeding and sale of dogs or engage in field-trial activities, the best advice is to think in terms of pedigree and registration. One caution regarding registration: Papers on your dog will not automatically produce an enthusiastic hunter. Nor will it insure easy training. It can serve as a confidence booster for you because it tells you the bloodline history. Often the issue is decided by the financial investment one is willing to make. Sad to report, I have often come across novice owners who mistakenly believe that a high price tag and papers guarantee easy training and competent hunting with a minimum of effort. There is no easy route to achieving the maximum potential of your dog. With papers or without, it will require considerable effort on your part.

Whichever you decide, the time has come to explore for prospective sellers. How do you know what to look for and how to minimize the risks in selecting your puppy? An inquiry to the American Kennel Club (AKC) can often prove invaluable. Among the information sources: veterinarians, other dog owners (especially Beagle owners), the local classified ads and national sporting publications. Regardless of which source you choose, it is absolutely imperative that you personally select your puppy at the kennel. Never purchase any dog sight unseen. The only time this cannot be avoided is if you are lucky enough to receive a puppy as a gift. This fortunate circumstance happened to me many years ago when I became acquainted with a young man who was working at a local grocery store. He and his father owned a number of Beagles and I was occasionally invited to hunt with him. My only dog at the time was getting along in years. The young man surprised me with a beautiful, female Beagle puppy as a birthday present. There was absolutely no way that I could have returned that beautiful puppy even if I had wanted to do so. I named her Bell and she became one of the finest "start" dogs I've ever owned. I hunted her the morning of the day she died at the age of 13 1/2. But getting a gift Beagle and making the most of it is not the usual situation. Here we want to focus on what to look for in selecting a puppy on your own.

You have decided to purchase your first puppy. The question of registered pedigree has been settled. You have dedicated and committed yourself to training sessions of at least one hour per week for the new addition. You have located a potential seller. Make an appointment with the seller, but check a couple of references before you go. If you are dealing with a reputable dealer who maintains a large kennel, he will be prepared to answer your many questions. If you are meeting with an individual who just happens to have a litter of puppies available, you can often check him out through acquaintances, friends or perhaps pet dealers.

Ask the Right Question

While selecting a puppy, it is amazing how often a potential buyer will suddenly become stricken with a case of lockjaw and purchase a puppy as though he were a pair of hunting socks. Remember, you are not buying a temporary gadget. You are trying to select a hunting companion who is likely to become a very important part of your life. In most cases, good common sense, judgment ability and your best instincts will get you through the selection process in good shape. Here is a list of questions to ask and some tips that should prove helpful in your dealings with the potential seller:

1. Who are the dam (mother) and sire (father)? Are they available for viewing? The reason for this question should be obvious. You are purchasing a Beagle puppy. No other breed will do. If possible, look at the parents to validate in your mind the kind of stock the puppy is coming from. It is also wise to look at certain traits of the parents, such as conformation, color, and disposition, since these are often passed to the offspring.

2. What is the hunting experience of the parents, including number of years and the type of game? Again, we are looking at heredity factors for hunting potential. If mom and dad were consistent hunters, particularly for rabbits, the chances are pup is going to inherit some of those genes. If one or both parents were used exclusively for deer hunting, the hunting genes are still there and training exclusively for rabbits is generally not impeded. On the other hand, if mom and dad both were exclusively family pets or show dogs with no proven hunting experience, your puppy can learn to become a successful hunting companion by following the proper training techniques.

3. Is there an opportunity to see one or both parents in a hunting situation? This will not always be possible. How-

ever, if a "race" or hunt can be arranged before purchase, it is a big plus. Many sellers do not have the facilities or the time for a trial run, but if the opportunity becomes available, by all means you should jump at the chance. It will reap many rewards. Remember that you are concerned with hunting bloodlines and the probability that the traits of the parents will be passed on to your puppy. You should note such things as "tongue" or the sound of the dog's bark, consistency on the game, starting ability and cooperation with other dogs. Starting ability is the dog's skill to look for game and begin barking when he finds the scent line. Other qualities to seek are trail sense, enthusiasm, disposition with people, general handling and behavior. The last of these traits, general handling and behavior, can be trained and will be discussed more thoroughly in another chapter. However, if you detect these favorable traits in either of the parents, there is a good chance that your puppy will inherit as least some of them.

4. What is the medical history of the parents? Are any major physical impairments visible? Depending upon conditions in your locale, a question about any history of heartworms, distemper, and parvovirus would all be significant. If you intend to become involved in breeding and selling, questions about such diseases as hip dysplasia would be in order. The seller may not have this information available, but if he does he should not hesitate to discuss it with you.

5. What is the medical history of the puppy, if any? At what age was he weaned? How old is he now? At this point, a note of caution is needed about weaning. Most puppies are weaned at six to eight weeks of age. If weaned earlier, the pup can suffer from malnutrition, which leads to all sorts of subsequent physical problems. Has he been started on a worming program? Has he received any vaccinations? Has he been seen by a veterinarian for any reason? If so, when, why and who was the vet? Does the seller have a medical record on the pup and is he will-

ing to furnish you with a copy? Most reputable breeders will gladly furnish all such records upon request.

6. What brand and type of food is the seller feeding the pup (if weaning has been completed)? You are not attempting to see if the seller is cutting costs by buying a less expensive feed. You want to establish consistency in feeding the pup when you get him home. This is a critical question because some dogs, especially puppies, cannot tolerate abrupt changes in their diets. It is better to err on the side of caution. If pup is used to eating Brand A dry dog food, the last thing you want to do is take him home and immediately feed him Brand B canned food, if that is your personal choice of feed. Just be certain to ask the seller the type and brand he is currently using. If you aren't positive that you can purchase that food in your locality, ask the seller where his supplier is located so you can continue with the same feed. Most sellers will gladly help you maintain the same diet. Often you can purchase enough from him to tide your puppy over until you can make other arrangements. Failure to inquire about the pup's diet can result in a very sick puppy or, even worse, the unnecessary death of your new puppy.

General Things to Watch For

Kennel Hygiene. Does the kennel look clean? Is there an excessive amount of feces littering the floor? What type of flooring is used? Dirt? Concrete? Other? Is the kennel generally well kept or is it unsightly? Is it in good repair? Is water available? Does it look fresh? Is it available to all dogs in the pen or kennel?

Shelter type and condition. Are the houses clean and in good repair? Is their evidence of roof leaks? Is there evidence of protection from weather extremes? Are straw or openings placed in ways that minimize drafts?

What is the effect of the owner on his dogs? Do they enjoy his presence? Does he enjoy being near and around them? Is he gentle? Do his dogs greet him enthusiastically or in quiet acceptance? Or do they shrink away and appear intimidated? Is he loud and obnoxious with them or do they appear to accept his presence?

What does the general appearance of all the dogs present tell you? Healthy? Satisfied? Energetic? Or are they lethargic, withdrawn, tired, underfed or ill looking?

Are the mother and litter kept separate from other dogs? Or are they crowded together in a helter-skelter fashion? Are they running free with no apparent pen or kennel?

Does the owner speak about his dogs with pride, respect and understanding? When he speaks to them, do you see him in control of himself and in control of them?

In talking with him about a potential puppy, does he guarantee this puppy to hunt? If so, use extreme caution

The grand review. Courtesy of Roger Brand, Walnut Ridge, Arkansas.

Two keys to selection are inquisitiveness and curiosity. Courtesy of Roger Brand.

unless he is willing to reduce such a claim to writing in the form of a contract. No one, especially an experienced dog man, would predict, much less guarantee, the future action of a puppy.

In general, be aware of how the seller handles himself and his dogs. Conditions are rarely perfect, but getting answers to these questions before making a final decision should help you make the right decision.

The Grand Review

Fewer things are more beautiful and emotion provoking to the dedicated dog enthusiast than a litter of healthy, energetic, playful Beagle puppies. The pups are so beautiful and adorable that you can be overwhelmed by the electricity they generate. Perhaps it is because such a viewing brings out the kid in all of us. Or perhaps a deeper psychological need is being met. Whatever the reason, this is the big moment!

It is often helpful to have someone accompany you at this time, providing that person has been through the puppy-selection process be-

Always consider the pup's comfort and security. Photo courtesy of Anderson's Big Creek Kennels, Jonesboro AR.

fore. If your companion is also a novice, his role should be relegated to that of moral supporter. Often as not, the companion will reaffirm your choice, providing you with a measure of self-confidence.

Ask the owner which of the puppies are actually for sale. Often the owner has previously promised one or more pups to others or plans to keep them himself. Whatever the case, ask the owner if he would allow the puppies out of the pen for a few minutes. If some of the puppies have been previously obligated, those can remain inside. If they are let out with the balance of the litter, you will have to go through the mental process of eliminating them as prospects. While the puppies are outside the pen, look very carefully at each one. Pick out those who are inquisitive and curious because these are primary hunting traits. Watch very carefully for those who keep their noses to the ground. Usually, these will be the same ones that exhibit the curiosity and inquisitiveness. Throughout this part of the process, there will be some puppies who will be primarily interested in playing with one another or seeking attention of whoever is in the vicinity. Beware of any puppy that appears listless or disinterested. This puppy may lack the maturity for training or, even worse, may be ill.

Let's return to those puppies who have their noses to the ground most of the time. These need your special attention because they have provided a clue toward selection of a potential hunter. It is perhaps the single most important selection key. The puppy with his nose on the ground is exhibiting the natural instinct to hunt and trail. These traits are absolutely essential in training and hunting.

You have now narrowed your choice to those select few. Some will be further eliminated by your previous decision to select a male or female. There will probably be very few puppies remaining. Your next step is to look at conformation and markings. In other words, does he look like a Beagle? Is he built like a Beagle? Does the pup look generally healthy? Are his movements unrestricted? Does his coat look healthy? In a standing or walking position, does he appear to have balance? Does his skin show a looseness that will allow him room to grow? Are his feet in good shape? Does he look and act like a hunter? Does he exhibit a pleasing personality? Pick him up. Does he seem to like you? Pet him. Does he respond to your touch and voice in a positive manner? Put him down. Let him wander off a few feet. Kneel and call, "Here, Puppy," several times if necessary. What is his response? Does he come within a minute or so? Or is he preoccupied to the point that he totally ignores you? When he comes to you, does he appear to enjoy being near or with you? Is he generally friendly or does he shrink from you and others? He should display a touch of boldness yet show affection.

These puppies have a healthy appetite. Photo courtesy of Anderson's Big Creek Kennels, Jonesboro AR.

Frequently, the question is asked whether one should select the runt of the litter. Ultimately, size shouldn't make a great deal of difference if the puppy meets the other important criteria. Likewise, there are arguments about selecting a puppy with only a dark-roofed mouth or one that shows flecks of brown on white in the coloring. There may or may not be something to these factors, but they appear to be matters of personal preference that do not affect a dog's ability to hunt.

The process described in this chapter was used in my selection of Sam, who was one of the best dogs I've owned. He was not registered but met most of the above criteria. He was 14 weeks old at the time of purchase and was a superb trail dog. He was an excellent hunting companion through the nearly 10 years I owned him before his death. He had one remarkable and unusual trait that is seldom exhibited or expected in the Beagle bloodline. He was a fabulous retriever of wounded rabbits. He had the uncanny ability to find a wounded rabbit, dispatch it with a quick snap of his jaws and return it to the gunner— regardless of the obstacles that could bar the return, be they water-filled ditches, ice-covered swamps or barbed-wire fencing.

This is not to say that your puppy will become a retrieving Beagle like Sam. However, it does reflect the logic of carefully following the selection process as closely as possible. Keep in mind that the process is only a guide. There are many variables, and your pup may not be an inferior choice because one or two of the criteria cannot be met. The process does, however, take some of the guesswork out of one of the most important aspects of Beagling. If you start with good material, the building process will be a little easier.

Chapter 2
Kennel Facilities And Maintenance

Your new addition can easily be kept in a secure wire mesh pen approximately 15 by 10 by 6 feet high. Some breeds require large runs, but Beagles adjust to such enclosures with relative ease. Proper attention to pen placement and the Beagle's comfort will accelerate the adjustment process, reduce stress and produce security for both you and pup. Experience has shown that, unlike bird-dog breeds, Beagles do not fare well on permanent yard chains. The Beagle personality and psychological makeup appear to require unrestricted movement. A secure pen provides him with unrestricted movement and satisfies his instinctive territorial needs. He feels protected and senses the enclosure is his home territory.

If you live in an apartment and don't have the space available, your only alternative is to house pup with you as a member of the family. This requires an entirely different approach, which includes house training and maintaining creature comforts. It is important, however, to maintain discipline wherever pup is housed. For our purposes, I am assuming you have adequate space in your yard for a small but secure pen.

Drainage

Constructing a 15x10x6 pen is not a major undertaking. It can be completed in a few hours with very little expense. However, in selecting a site, take special note of natural drainage. If the pen is constructed in a low-lying area where water is likely to stand for several hours, it is recommended that an adequate drainage system be installed. Ideally, the pen should be placed where there is good natural drainage, leaving pup

A pen with natural shade and drainage is important.

dry and secure. Although my own pen has natural drainage, I installed a drain system of three-inch PVC pipe with a four-inch drain cap. This provides for more convenient cleaning during the warm and hot summer months. Periodic hosing helps reduce odors and parasites.

Security

Special steps should be taken to make the pen puppy proof. Most dogs love to dig, perhaps out of boredom or natural instinct or both. So take precautions to ensure that the bottom edges of the pen are secured inside and out with bricks, lengths of 4x4 lumber or heavy blocks. If you choose to use the lengths of 4x4 lumber, nail or staple the wire mesh to them inside and out. If pup is going to escape, he will have to dig completely under the wire on both sides of the mesh. This rarely happens. As you make daily inspections of your pen, take note of fresh holes. A brick, rock or other heavy object placed in the fresh hole is usually sufficient to discourage pup from exploiting that particular area. Another device designed to thwart pup is called "hog proofing" the pen. This utilizes metal rods 12 inches long. One end is bent at an angle so that when the rod is pounded into the ground, the bottom of the mesh is caught on the angled portion and held flush with the ground. These are rarely necessary but can prevent the most energetic dog from digging his way out.

Shade

In placing the pen, take special note of available shade. Dogs do not sweat; they pant. A resting place in the shade is critical during hot summer days. If natural shade is not available you can install artificial shade, such as colored fiberglass panels, on the top of the pen so shade is available for at least part of the day. Do not use clear fiberglass because it magnifies the sun's rays. Also, consider planting a shade tree in a strategic location so that natural shade is eventually available. While you may have your own personal preference, I have found a species of the pecan tree serves this purpose well. In addition to providing shade, it attracts other wildlife species and you can enjoy harvesting the nuts each autumn.

In selecting building materials, you might want to consider chain link. However, if cost is a major consideration, wire mesh not exceeding two inches square works just fine. This prevents pup from getting his head through, thus reducing the risk of choking or injury. Once installed, if you find pup can still get his head through, install smaller mesh wire along the bottom and up the sides completely around the pen as a temporary barrier. Pup will learn to accept this barrier fairly quickly.

You will need to purchase nine or 10 one-inch angle iron posts seven or eight feet long. Setting these 10-to-12 inches into the ground should be adequate to hold the most active dog. A supply of flexible yet durable wire to tie the corners and mesh sections together will also be needed. It has been my experience that such a pen can be constructed by two untrained individuals in two to four hours. The pen need not be elaborate but it does need to be secure and durable. You are primarily concerned with providing security, preventing escape and reducing the risk of injury to the dog.

Partitioning

While construction is in progress, give serious consideration to partitioning the pen. This will require an additional post placed approximately one half the length of the pen or eight feet along the longest stretch of wire and about three feet inside for the installation of a gate. A partition is easy to install and can give you many advantages. The gate can be left open, allowing pup additional space and movement. If you increase the number of dogs, there are occasions when one or more of them will need to be separated, perhaps because of illness or injury. Or you may need to separate a bitch with a litter from the larger dogs or use the partition for weaning purposes. The partition will also come in handy when you need to make necessary pen repairs or perform major cleaning chores or renovation. The partition is not an absolute necessity, but the extra time and effort spent on installation will prove its worth. Finally, be sure pup is secure by padlocking the gate. Beagles are becoming more valuable every day and are often the target of thieves.

A pen that is partitioned offers many advantages.

Housing

Dog houses are as varied as the people who build them. It has been my experience that a dog house can cost more than all the pen facilities. So it pays to shop around. The house should be roomy but not drafty. Three feet by three feet by two feet in height will be sufficient for one or

A dog house with an incline serves two purposes.

even two dogs. The larger the house, the more insulation is needed to keep it warm and comfortable. Look for a house with an inclined or sloped roof covered with shingles. It is imperative to maintain drainage to prevent leaks. Flat box-type roofs are notorious for developing leaks. With a sloped roof, there will be rapid drainage of water and melting snow and ice. Also, an incline allows you to place pup atop the roof for periodic inspections. Most dogs fear heights, so pup is out of his element when he is put on top of the house for inspection. And this allows you more control of his actions.

If you are handy with tools, making a dog house requires little time and expense. Whether you purchased or build the house, be sure that the main entrance is large enough for access but not excessive.

For winter warmth and insulation, I recommend filling the house with straw purchased at your local feed store. Avoid cloth items such as old rags, rugs or cloths. Pup can easily drag these items into the pen yard where they become soiled and wet. He will often as not drag them back into the house in this condition, producing a dirty, damp floor and bedding area. Carpeting can be used inside the house if it is secured to the floor. However, it can be a problem when it becomes wet. Straw does the job best because it provides warmth and insulation in winter and can be easily removed in late spring or early summer.

It often amazes me that people will spend lavishly on their dog houses and then place them in a helter-skelter fashion. When locating your dog house, note the major weather patterns in your area and arrange for the main entrance to be placed away from the prevailing winds or at least not facing directly into them. For example, if the strongest weather fronts come from the southwest, arrange the house so the main entrance faces northeast or away from those prevailing winds. This will reduce drafts and contribute to pup's overall comfort. He deserves as much. The house should be elevated on bricks or blocks to prevent premature deterioration and enhance dryness.

Pen Flooring

There are several types of pen floors you will want to consider. Like many other things in life, cost may be the deciding factor. Initially, dirt may take precedence simply because the costs of concrete, chat and other materials are financially out of reach. All types of flooring have advantages and disadvantages, as follows:

Dirt Floors. A dirt floor provides pup a natural surface for his feet to develop, and it is a well-known fact that dogs enjoy digging. A dirt floor allows pup to dig a hole or, in most cases, a series of them, during the hot summer months to obtain a cool place to combat the heat. The digging action helps to keep his toenails worn down to a proper length and helps him in natural muscle development as well. The holes can be filled quickly only to be dug again and again.

The obvious disadvantages are problems of keeping pup clean, infestation of parasites and the creation of standing water in the pen. Standing water attracts mosquitoes, which in turn increases the risk of heartworms, an especially serious problem in the South and Southeastern sections of the country. Nevertheless, dirt flooring is not all negative and many dog owners have and never would consider anything else.

Chat and Gravel. The advantage to using chat and/or gravel is that pup can develop toughness in his feet and pads. It is also easy to maintain and clean. On the negative side, while it can help in the development of feet and pad toughness, it can result in wear and tear on pup's feet. It is perhaps a good choice, providing pup gets adequate time in the field to develop other leg muscles and ligaments. Daily runs in the field can reduce foot problems while pup lives on chat and/or gravel, but many owners do not have the time or space for daily exercises. If you have the time and space for a minimum of every-other-day runs, chat and/or gravel would be an excellent choice.

Concrete. Concrete flooring is probably the best all-around flooring for Beagles. It is clean, provides good parasite control and is easy and convenient to clean and maintain. It is however, the most expensive type of flooring, hardly a minor consideration. Some veterinarians do not recommend concrete flooring for heavier breeds because their weight places additional pressure on their feet, resulting in splayed feet. For Beagles, this is not usually a problem. If you have the means and expertise to lay the concrete, I highly recommended that you do so. As with any hard-surface pen flooring, frequent foot inspections are recommended. Concrete dust can be extremely painful if pup happens to have a cut on his foot and dust enters the open wound. Frequent foot inspections should be part of your routine regardless of flooring, but it is especially important when hard surfaces are used.

Brick Flooring. Brick flooring is a good all-around compromise. It has the advantage of parasite control, easy cleaning and maintenance, and relatively low cost if you can acquire sufficient supplies. Keep in mind that used brick is usually more expensive than new, molded brick. It sounds illogical but my experience shows this to be the case.

After many years of keeping my dogs on dirt flooring, I arrived at brick flooring as a good alternative. My inclination to stretch a dollar led me to keep watch for old burned-out houses both in town and in the country on my numerous trips to hunting sites. I was able to locate a site and secure permission from the owner to haul enough bricks to establish a floor in my pen. I sent the owner a small check along with a note of appreciation. Although I wasn't an expert brick layer, I was able to seal most of the cracks with mortar and now have a solid floor that is easy to hose down and maintain. My dogs are relatively free of parasites and appear quite content. The cost was minimal. It is an option I highly recommend.

Wire Mesh. Wire mesh flooring is generally used in cages, which in turn are placed within the pen enclosure itself. While it is a modified system, I've seen them used. The cages are usually about 3 1/2 feet off the ground and are approximately five feet long. A small shelter or house is installed in the rear. Owners who have this type of arrangement appear quite happy with it. My experience with this arrangement is quite limited, so I will withhold a recommendation. However, it is an option you may want to consider.

Water and Feeding Arrangements

When placing water supplies, remember pup is small and can only reach a certain height. Placing his water source in a 12-inch, 2 1/2-gallon bucket is going to be ridiculous if his maximum height reach is only seven or eight inches. Consider two water sources in case pup gets playful and pulls one over. You might consider using a small dish for immediate access plus a large bucket that he can lie next to for cooling purposes during the hot summer days. The important factor is to provide fresh, clean water every day. During hot days, water should be changed twice a day. It takes little time and pup will appreciate your effort.

For feeding purposes, prevent waste by selecting a bowl that allows pup to reach the contents easily without turning it over. Some owners elect to install automatic feeders but I avoid these systems. Pup needs and wants to know who his master is. If you are like most of us working folk, there is precious little time for the finer things in life such as time with family and friends. Likewise, there is little time for our dogs. Over the years, I've attempted to make feeding time a special time between my dogs and myself. Take advantage of feed time to get to know pup. You can learn a lot about him in just a few minutes of petting, encouraging and instilling basic discipline. What better time than mealtime? Pup is a creature of habit, much as you and I. He expects you to feed him. He expects you to water him. He expects you to discipline him if necessary. So, the daily feeding and watering become more than simply providing the basic necessities. These chores enhance the companionship and understanding that needs to take place between you. Taking advantage of mealtime will pay dividends during the later training periods.

The pen, regardless of flooring, should be kept as clean as possible. Daily scooping and proper disposal of feces helps prevent unpleasant odors and helps pup keep his feet clean. Consider obtaining a scoop-type shovel or a long-handled scooper for this chore. There are several good ones on the market. Deposit the waste in five-gallon plastic buckets with air-tight tops and bails. These can often be acquired from a local restaurant (used as pickle containers) or restaurant supply company. They are extremely durable and will last for years. When the buckets are near full, they can easily be taken to a landfill or other suitable disposal site, emptied and returned. These buckets hold a surprising amount of waste, and times between emptying can be quite long.

The advantage to solid flooring with adequate drainage is that residual waste can be hosed down on a daily basis during the warm months, eliminating unpleasant odors and adding to pup's comfort and contentment.

Frequent inspection of your pen is important. Keep a close eye out for nails, sharp sticks or other items that might accidentally injure the pup. Dispose of these immediately. A minute spent to eliminate the hazard can save pup a lot of pain and you an expensive vet bill.

Disinfection and odor control can be accomplished easily if you have a solid pen floor. Personally, I use liquid bleach, splashed on the floor. Then I sweep it clean with a broom. Finally, I rinse and flush the excess. This is done twice a month during the summer months. Liquid bleach can also be used to disinfect feed, water bowls and dog houses. Simply mix two parts bleach for each gallon of water. It also helps in controlling parasites.

In building and maintaining a kennel, the main consideration is pup's comfort and security. You will be asking a lot from him in the coming months and years. He will be working long and hard to please you without a single complaint. Keeping him well housed is one way you can do to show your appreciation for his efforts.

Chapter 3
Adjustments And General Care

Those First Few Days

You now have pup at home. Your kennel has been checked for security. Hazardous objects have been removed. The dog house is clean, dry and warm. Water is available and accessible. The food bowl is full. Put pup down. Talk to him in a soothing tone of voice. Encourage him to investigate. Remember, this is foreign territory to him and he is anxious and probably frightened. So spend a few minutes with him while he tries to get his bearings. Encourage him to locate the food and water. If he hesitates to enter the dog house, gently help him inside.

I suggest that you get an old article of your clothing, preferably unwashed, to leave with him. Place it in the dog house or in the pen so it is available to him. Remember, he knows who you are because you have been the primary handler throughout the selection process and during the trip home. He is beginning to respond to your voice and, more importantly, to your scent. This discarded article of clothing will serve as his security blanket for the first few days. If he can't see you, at least he can smell you. This will also help reduce much of the irritating and often frustrating whining and barking that is commonplace during those first few days.

If you are placing him with other dogs, watch carefully for any hostile reactions. Generally, there is a lot of sniffing, smelling, and tail wagging. Acceptance is usually a simple process. However, some dogs will not readily accept a new dog because of their territorial instincts, and pup just might be considered an intruder. This is when the partitioned pen is especially handy. Just keep pup isolated from the others for two or three days until the others can determine for themselves that he poses no threat. Then reintroduce him to the others.

In most cases, one of the older dogs, particularly a bitch, will protect and mother him, thus eliminating any undue risks. A pecking order will eventually be established by the dogs in their own way.

Feeding Considerations

One of the more difficult problems with placing pup with other dogs immediately is insuring that he has sufficient access to food and water without competition from the others. Again, the pen that has been partitioned solves this problem. Let him work out his own place in the hierarchy, but feed him separately. Eventually, he will adjust to their feeding schedule and learn his place at the feed bowl. But during those first few weeks, it is important he be fed not less than twice a day to allow for maximum development and growth. Proper feeding cannot be over-emphasized.

The type of feed and the portions are no less important than making feeding a special time. To argue the merits of one brand of feed versus another is useless for our purposes. However, be cautioned about selecting a product because it looks good to you. Many people reject a good, basic feed because "it doesn't look good to eat," and their dog suffers as a result. There are many excellent brands on the market. My favorite product happens to be a dry feed that helps reduce tooth tartar and is convenient to use. Most importantly, it meets the requirements of the Association of American Feed Control Officials (AAFCO). Check the label and look for a listing of the following nutrients and whether the feed meets or exceeds the AAFCO requirements. The following nutrients should be listed: Protein, Fat, Linolic Acid, Calcium, Phosphorous, Potassium, Sodium Chloride, Magnesium, Iron, Copper, Manganese, Zinc, Iodine, Selenium, Vitamins A, D, and E, Thiamine, Riboflavin, Pantothenic Acid, Niacin, Pyridoxine, Folic Acid, Biotin, Vitamin B12, and Choline.

How do you know you are getting what the label says? That could only be proven by a series of chemistry tests. Not being a qualified chemist, I can only judge the quality of the feed by the performance of my dogs. I've been quite satisfied with this brand and my dogs' performance for more than a dozen years.

Keep pup's feeding schedule on a regular basis.

Remember to continue pup with the same feed on which he was weaned. If you are feeding a dry food, usually 16 ounces served once in the morning and once in the evening will be sufficient initially. Check the label for the manufacturer's recommendation, if provided. If you are switching pup to a different brand, begin with a five-day changeover schedule. The first day feed four-fifths the original feed mixed with one-fifth of the new brand. On day two, feed three-fifths of the original and two-fifths of the new brand. Continue this one-fifth-a-day gradual change for three more days. Watch for any changes in pup's stools and physical condition. If you spot signs of trouble, revert to the previous day's formula and remain there until all abnormal signs disappear. Then continue with the changeover schedule as described. If all goes well, pup should be handling his new diet without problems after five to seven days. If serious problems develop, check with your veterinarian. Remember, pup's system needs time to adjust. Abrupt changes in diet can result in the unnecessary and tragic loss of a fine dog. Although older dogs are not as susceptible to adverse reactions to feed changes, the five-day changeover is recommended for them as well.

Two feedings a day should continue until pup no longer needs them. How will you know when pup no longer needs them? Just keep an eye on his bowl. When you begin to notice that he does not clean up his bowl between feeding times, that's usually a good indication that once-a-day feedings are about to arrive. I generally continue with two feedings for a while, decreasing the amount in the morning for several days. Then I switch completely to one feeding a day. This system has always worked very satisfactorily for my dogs. One problem with dry feed is keeping it fresh. This problem can be solved quite easily by storing it in a metal 25-gallon trash can. Be sure the can has a solid, airtight lid.

Pup's feeding schedule should be consistent and maintained on a regular basis as far as practical. Pup is like us in this respect. Most of you work, sleep, bathe, eat, etc., on a routine schedule. At times, circumstances require that you modify your schedule, but that's the exception rather than the rule. Pup needs his schedule as well. If you feed him at five each evening, try to maintain that schedule. If you opt for a morning feeding, that's perfectly proper. The time of day is less important than the consistency. Frankly, I prefer an evening feed time because if I'm going to run pup for chase or hunt, he will have voided himself the previous night before being place in the carrier box. This eliminates obvious problems during transportation.

Is it okay to feed table scraps? There's no easy answer, and it's a yes and no proposition. Pup cannot be expected to perform at an optimum level if his diet is mostly inferior. Put another way, you can't expect the most out of him if you put the wrong things into him. Table scraps have their place as long as you maintain his proper nutritional level. However, some scraps are taboo, including fish and chicken bones. Chicken bones are basically hollow. When pup crunches down on one, he risks getting a splinter lodged in his throat. Fish bones are needle sharp and can damage pup's mouth and throat. These bones do a disservice to pup, so avoid them. I personally avoid feeding pork and venison bones as well. Well-cooked beef or grease mixed with dry food can add flavor and variety to pup's meal. During cold, winter days or when pup is working extra hard in the field, a spoonful of pure lard, grease and/or white bread items, given with his feed, have a tendency to help keep his energy level up. So, yes, scraps are acceptable. But use discretion. Pup is like you and will eat a lot of things because he likes them. That does not necessarily mean they are good for him.

During the first few days of pup's adjustment, you will need to fit him with a collar. The sooner the better. Pup needs to get used to a collar because it's going to become pretty much a permanent fixture. For his first collar, avoid the those that are heavily oiled. They won't hurt him or you, but puppies have a way of getting them loose enough to chew on them. The more he tastes, the more he chews. Also avoid a star or ornamental studded collar. If he should slip one of these off his neck, the chewing action may cause damage to his mouth.

A plain adjustable collar is best. When you place it on him, allow it to be loose enough for you to slip two fingers easily between the collar and his skin, but snug enough that it won't slip over his head. Later, when he is five to six months old, you will need to change to a collar that allows you to affix an identification plate to it. This can be accomplished by the use of split brads of brass or copper. You can do this job easily yourself or have it done at your local shoe-repair shop. It is imperative that the tag plate include your name and phone number. Some states require all hunting dogs to be properly identified in this manner, so be sure to check your local hunting regulations. Some owners have their dogs tattooed for additional identification. At the very least, get the plate on the collar. It can save you and pup a lot of anguish if pup gets lost.

The First Veterinarian Visit

At the earliest date possible, make an appointment for pup with your veterinarian. It's time for pup to see the doctor, a key figure in pup's life. What follows is a discussion about what can be generally expected at pup's first visit. Most veterinarians are very patient and understanding. The veterinarians I've known are highly skilled professionals who are always ready to answer questions, so don't be afraid to ask questions concerning your pup's health. You will want to ask about vaccinations and de-worming procedures in particular.

Vaccinations. Vaccinations are not cures. They are preventive measures against certain types of diseases to which pup is susceptible. Most vets prefer to start vaccinations when puppies are six to eight weeks old. These are repeated every three weeks until about the 16th week. Along with the beginning vaccinations pup can expect to undergo stool and blood tests. The vaccinations will include distemper, a disease most dogs are exposed to during their lives. Distemper is a killer, so this vaccination is an absolute necessity.

Coronavirus is a stomach infection that if left untreated can also result in death. So pup will get this vaccination as well. Leptspnosis or "Lepto" affects the kidneys. Pup will receive a vaccination for this as well as for canine cough. Parvovirus, a devastating disease that can be transmitted through direct contact with the feces of infected dogs, is prevented only through vaccines. Canine Hepatitis is another killer, so pup will receive a vaccination for this as well.

Most of these vaccines are combined, making it unnecessary for pup to get a separate inoculation for each one. Your vet can provide you with specific information on the combinations. The important thing to remember is that all of the vaccinations are critical to pup's health.

Finally, pup will get his rabies vaccination. Some vets prefer to wait until the sixth or seventh month before administering this vaccine. However, it is absolutely critical pup receive this inoculation. In the field, pup will be exposed to many different critters and one never knows when an episode with a rabid skunk, raccoon or other carrier might occur. Whether the vet vaccinates pup early or late, it is critical for him (and you) to receive this protection. Most state laws require a rabies vaccination and the vet will provide you with a metal tag with an imprinted number. While the vet will maintain a permanent record of this number and the date, it is also a good idea to record the information in pup's health record at home. Rabbit dogs are notorious for loosing their collars and thus their tags. Keep the number and date of vaccination handy.

After pup is a year old, he will need annual booster shots for distemper, parvovirus and rabies. If you need additional information, check with your vet.

De-Worming. When pup is eight to ten weeks old, it will be necessary to begin a regular de-worming program for hook, tape, round and ring worms. You will need to de-worm pup every 90 days by administering a combination pill based on pup's weight. These pills can be obtained from your vet, pet supply or feed store. Administer the first pill and record the date. The second pill should be administered 10 to 14 days later. It is easy to forget the dates so this is a good time to establish a health record booklet for pup. Some vets provide these upon request. My booklet is a small, simple, notebook in which I keep a record of vaccinations, rabies tag number, date of birth, weights, worming dates and all vet visits. This record is easy to maintain and helps to reduce the risk of over-worming. It also provides me with pup's health profile at a glance.

Pup will need a heartworm program at about eight to 10 weeks. Your vet will help you choose either a daily or monthly program. You will want to discuss this with him. The vet will perform a routine blood test to determine whether pup is a carrier of the worm larvae. This is necessary because if the test results are positive, pup cannot be placed on the medications. If the results are negative, his prevention program starts immediately and he will need to be kept on a regular routine. Check with your vet on his recommendations for follow-up tests.

While pup is visiting the doctor, he will receive a routine physical exam that includes a check of the eyes, ears, nose, mouth, body/coat, anus, feet and legs. This is an ideal time to ask the vet any questions you may have on your mind. The only dumb question is the one that isn't asked. Your vet will be glad to answer them.

Get to know your vet. He is a hard working professional who can be a critical part of pup's life. Ask him who takes his calls when he unavailable. Most vets have agreements with other veterinarians to cover their calls during an absence. If you are planning to be out of town and are leaving pup in someone else's care, talk to your vet about the handling of emergencies while you are away. Secure his approval for pup to be seen on an emergency basis should the need arise. Work out financial arrangements with him so he is assured of payment. I prefer to patronize a veterinarian who will allow an emergency visit in my absence, upon my notifying him of the dates, and allow me to be billed later for the service. Always inform those who care for pup of these arrangements and provide them with the vet's name and phone number. This type of arrangement minimizes misunderstandings and safeguards the dog's well being.

Control of Parasites. Aside from worms, pup will acquire some other very unpleasant critters who view him as the main dinner course— primarily fleas and ticks. Total eradication is nearly impossible, but you owe it to pup to wage war on these rascals. Fleas and ticks have been around longer than mankind and there appears little chance they will vacate the planet any time soon.

Ticks dig into pup's skin and feed on his blood. Given current information regarding Lyme Disease, precaution is necessary when removing a tick found embedded in pup's hide. If you are compelled to remove one by hand, it is recommended that you wear protective gloves.

There are many fine products available in the form of dips, sprays and powders designed to help reduce and control ticks. Regular inspection of pup's coat can reveal any tick infestation. An application of either a dip, spray or powder will go a long way toward helping you control these parasites.

Fleas are extremely difficult to control. This is because they become immune to a particular product after a year or two. This means you should be prepared to switch products frequently just to maintain a level battlefield in the war on fleas.

Fleas and ticks are most prevalent during spring and summer. Even if pup is penned most of the time, these parasites can make life miserable for him. A good flea and tick shampoo, administered twice a month with a small stiff-bristle brush in a number two galvanized washtub, does wonders for pup. Dips and powders are also valuable weapons, but shampoos appear to be most effective.

If your pen has a solid floor, either brick or concrete, wash it down with liquid bleach. Then spread a good powder liberally on the floor and inside the dog house. Even if the pen floor is dirt or chat, the powdering operation should be performed at least every two weeks. Fleas and ticks bed primarily in dirt, and it's a constant battle to keep them in check.

During cold weather, inspect pup's coat frequently by running your hand in the direction opposite to the grain of his hair. This will reveal most fleas or ticks. If any are found, administer a good tick/flea powder. Be sure to powder the inside of his house and his favorite outside resting places. Generally, fleas and ticks are less of a problem during cold winter months, but you can bet they will be back in full force when the weather turns warm. Remember that precautions should always be taken when using any chemical. Read the label before using any of these products, and follow the directions. If you are in doubt whether they will harm you or pup, contact your vet.

Are his toenails too long?

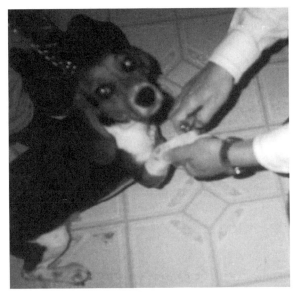

Regular Inspections. Inspect pup frequently for his general health. Look at his feet. Are there any objects wedged between his toes, such as burrs or caked dirt? Removal of these items is not a major undertaking.

If a burr is lodged in the hair, you might need to use scissors to clip a few hairs before gently lifting out the burr. Caked dirt can usually be removed with your fingers or, if necessary, with some warm water.

Are his pads in good shape? Do you find any small cuts or abrasions? If so, clean and treat them with an antiseptic to prevent possible infection.

Are his toenails too long? Do they extend far beyond the pad into a curling-back position? If so, you will need to trim them with a high-quality nail clipper purchased from your local pet-supply store. Caution should be taken that the nails not be trimmed too short because the toenail contains blood. If you are not sure you can do the job, your vet or his assistant will usually do it for a small fee. Some dogs grow toenails like garden weeds and require frequent clippings. Others require infrequent clipping, perhaps only once a year. As pup gets older and hunts hard, he will probably experience a pulled toenail. This is not an uncommon problem for Beagles, as they are constantly encountering honeysuckle vines, barbed wire, and a variety of roots and briars. An extended toenail snags and sometimes pulls loose. Keeping pup's toenails in good shape can help prevent or at least minimize these injuries.

A fiberglass carrier makes a hassle-free transport.

Inspect his coat. Does it appear glossy and healthy? Are there bare spots? This might indicate excessive scratching caused by fleas or possibly the onset of mange.

Assess his weight. Has he lost weight? Does he look thin? This might indicate worms or even more serious problems. Look at his eyes. Do they look clear? Or is there excessive matter in the corners?

Most Beagle owners have their favorite antiseptics for small cuts and abrasions. I prefer a brand called *Doctor Tichinor's Antiseptic*. After applying it with a cotton ball or cotton swab, allow it to dry for about a minute. Then tannic acid, otherwise known as *Blue Ointment*, is applied. This combination has, through the years, prevented infection in any of my dogs' minor cuts and abrasions. If you are unsure of the proper medication or procedure for any injury, consult your veterinarian.

Travel and Transportation. Transporting pup can often be a gigantic hassle. Just like some people, pup might suffer from motion sickness. If pup travels in the family car and gets one of his sick spells, neither you nor he will be very popular with other members of the family—especially if Junior happens to have a date that night and you have promised him use of the car. Only after plenty of cleaning and deodorizing will the vehicle be fit for human use.

You could lock pup in the trunk of the car, but often as not he is just going to become more sick and frightened. You could put him in the cargo bay of your pickup truck and tie him to something, but at the very least you would subject him to the risk of eye damage from the wind. And there would be the risk of major injury if pup slips his collar or manages to reach the side of the truck. Another alternative is to build a wooden carrier box, but often the weight of the box can pose the risk of hernia when you attempt to lift and load it.

After experiencing most of the these mishaps over a period of years, I've hit on a clean, no hassle, convenient, relatively inexpensive and safe method of transporting dogs. Here's how it works:

For a small investment of 30 to 45 dollars, depending on local prices, you should be able to purchase a fiberglass pet carrier similar to those used by commercial airlines. These carriers can be obtained at most major department stores and pet shops, or they can be ordered through sporting goods stores or outlets. The carriers are very durable, generally composed of lightweight fiberglass with mesh gates made from high-grade steel. They are simple to clean by wiping it out with a damp cloth in cold weather or hosing it down during warm weather.

When transporting by pickup truck during cold or cool weather, the carrier can be covered with a heavy canvas or tarp, which is tucked around the edges and anchored by enough two-by-four pieces to keep the canvas from blowing or flapping in the wind. Attaching a 10- or 12-foot yard chain through the side air vents and across the top allows the carrier to be fastened to the sides or bed of the truck and padlocked for security. This system keeps pup warm, comfortable, safe and secure.

If travel is by family automobile or other enclosed vehicle, simply place the carrier on the rear seat and place pup inside. If he becomes carsick, the mess will be confined to the carrier area. For easier cleanup, line the bottom of the carrier with newspaper. This can be easily discarded. It's amazing how quickly pup will learn not to soil his private box.

If motion sickness continues to be a real problem, take pup in his carrier box on short trips to the grocery store or other errands, preferably when his stomach is empty. After several trips over a time, he will generally get used to the box and no longer slobber or vomit. If the problem persists, consult your veterinarian.

Another advantage to this lightweight carrier is that it can be easily maneuvered for training purposes. (I will discuss this in a later chapter.) The carrier-and-canvas transportation system is very flexible and worth the small initial expense.

Before leaving the topic of general care, a further note on providing fresh water on a daily basis: During winter months, especially in colder areas of the country, freezing of pup's drinking water can be a major problem. Pup needs his water to prevent de-hydration regardless of the weather. Some owners purchase electrical systems that prevent freezeups. I've always been a bit skeptical of these systems for fear of accidental electrocution. I solved the problem by using a revolving bucket brigade requiring a pair of 2 1/2-gallon galvanized buckets. One is filled in the house or at an insulated outside faucet and placed in the pen. The other one remains empty inside the house. At feeding time, I fill the empty reserve bucket and replace the frozen bucket in the pen. The frozen bucket can be thawed in the house and left empty until the next feeding and watering time. This system assures pup of plenty of fresh water and eliminates excessive wear and tear on a single bucket. It may not be an elaborate, sophisticated system, but it works remarkably well.

Chapter 4
Before You Begin: Mental Preparation

For many years before owning my first Beagle, I hunted with other Beagle owners at every opportunity. I've always enjoyed hunting in general and rabbit hunting in particular. Those owners, recognizing my obvious enthusiasm, would occasionally ask me why I didn't have my own dog(s). I can recall responding with a variety of excuses such as "not enough time to fool with a dog" or "no place to keep one." Or I didn't have the money to buy a trained dog, which was partially true because trained Beagles are not inexpensive. The truth was I would have enjoyed owning a good rabbit dog but I just didn't know how to go about training a dog to hunt.

Occasionally, I would ask an owner how to go about training a dog to hunt rabbits and the general response was: "Oh, you just take him with you. He'll learn it on his own." So, when I received my first Beagle pup, Bell, I just took her with me for a couple of years. And guess what? She really did learn some things. She learned to chase other dogs, cats, squirrels and other game. And she learned to run away! Frustrated, I just hoped that eventually she would learn to hunt rabbits on her own if I took her into the field often enough.

In the meantime, she was rapidly developing some inappropriate behavior and was totally undisciplined. When she was put down to hunt, she would bolt and run as fast and as far as she could away from me. No amount of calling, pleading, begging or yelling would stop her—forget trying to call her in later. If I wanted her, I went and found her. When it was time to be leashed, she would struggle against the leash, resisting all my pleading. After a couple of years of this unpleasantness, I was about to pronounce her a general nuisance and get rid of her.

It was about that time I met Col. Joseph F. Chambers, (USAF, Ret.), a co-worker who became my mentor. An experienced Beagle man, Joe sometimes invited me on rabbit hunts. His dogs were well behaved, seemed easy to handle and consistently produced rabbits. I noted that he always knew the whereabouts of his dogs. There was no time wasted hunting for dogs. Time was devoted to hunting rabbits. In discussing my dog problems with him, he said: "Bill, you can't expect her to hunt if she doesn't know what you want her to hunt and how you want her to hunt it." Under Joe's guidance and direction, Bell became a fine rabbit dog. It wasn't that he took her and worked with her, rather it was his coaching me how to teach her what to do. I learned the valuable lesson that the trainer must train himself and know what he wants from his dog before his dog can be expected to perform. In short, I began to learn the process of "hand training" Beagles.

There are undoubtedly other ways to train Beagles, but as a novice owner/trainer this method should help you avoid many of the mistakes, pitfalls and problems I unfortunately had to endure with my first dog. Bell eventually became one of the best rabbit dogs a man could want but it was only because Joe Chambers took the time and effort to teach me.

To begin, you will need a measure of self-discipline to maintain a regular training routine for pup. You will need to commit yourself to at least one hour per week for training in the fundamentals. These funda-

Maintaining a regular training schedule requires discipline.

If you are upset, it's best to let pup have a playtime. Photo courtesy of Joe Chambers.

mentals begin in yard training and later carry over into field work. One of the problems of scheduling sessions is the inevitable conflict with all of your other obligations. However, most of you will generally find time to engage in the activities you most enjoy. It's a matter of setting priorities. As you begin to spend more time with pup, one hour per week won't seem quite as difficult as you first thought. As pup progresses, you will probably be tempted to extend the time period. That's all well and good, but a word of caution here. Limit the actual training exercises to no more than one hour. At any rate, set a goal of one hour per week and commit yourself to it. You might have to sacrifice a portion of that Saturday or Sunday afternoon television football game, but it will be worth it as you begin to see pup's progress.

Remember, pup learns very little, if anything, confined in the kennel. He learns nothing about hunting if he isn't provided the opportunity. And he is totally dependent on you to provide those opportunities. If you commit yourself to the goal of one hour per week, you enhance the reality of achieving pup's potential. If you cannot make this commitment, you will do pup a real injustice and perhaps you need to re-think your decision to undertake the task.

Prepare yourself to be patient. You are all endowed with a measure of patience, but some of you have a larger capacity for it than others. The key is to remember that patience is a learned attribute. If you are one who has a shallow capacity for it, you will need to train yourself to keep your cool when pup pays absolutely no attention to your instructions. Patience allows you to keep control of pup's actions and the entire training situation.

When you begin to lose your patience, simply back away mentally. Just stop what you are doing for a few moments until you can regain your composure and self control. Generally, you lose patience with pup because you have psychologically set your expectations of him too high. You want him to excel and he isn't performing at your expected levels.

Be consistent in all your communications with pup. Inconsistency in verbal commands and actions will only confuse him, resulting in wasted time and effort. For example, you want pup to come to you so you cheerfully give the command "come;" then when he finally comes, you scold him for some previous misbehavior. Pup can't understand why he is being scolded. He was simply attempting to obey the first command he was given. The next time he hears the come command he will expect to be scolded and therefore will hesitate to respond. When you give the command "stay" because you want him to remain in place and wait for you, don't suddenly change the command to "wait." There is a chance he will stay for a minute or two, but he probably will go on about his business because he doesn't understand the wait command. He understands stay, not wait. So always be consistent in your verbal commands. Once pup learns to respond to them, never change them. To do so confuses him through no fault of his own.

"Keep it simple" is an excellent motto when training pup. Neither you nor pup needs to be a mental giant to achieve your goals. There is no need to complicate things. Ultimately, you as the trainer will control pup's actions, but keep it simple. Give simple, one-word commands. There is no need to explain things to him because he isn't going to understand. He simply reacts to your voice, body language and scent. He will, through repetition, learn to carry out those commands you give him if you keep them simple and use them often enough that the actions become a matter of habit.

What you are attempting to do is to establish actions in pup that are based on habits and formed through repetition. You are doing this so pup will learn to perform at his maximum level. You are attempting to establish control through handling to develop pup's positive traits to their highest levels and prevent undesirable conduct.

To establish control, you need to be persistent. Often, pup will be distracted. But you, as the controller and trainer, must be prepared to repeat

Always reward pup for good performance and behavior within 30 seconds.

the request or command as many times as necessary for pup to develop the proper habit or action, even when he prefers to do otherwise. Beagle training probably can best be described as one step forward and two steps backwards. Sometimes it will seem as though you just are not getting through to pup and his progress is painfully slow. Remember that pup's attention span is very short. When he performs as you command, reward him with lavish praise or edibles or both immediately, no later than 30 seconds after the completed action. If you fail to do this, he will miss the point of the command entirely. The 30-second reward rule is a critical element in training, whether associated with positive or negative commands. So don't delay. While pup can absorb a tremendous amount of information, he lacks the capacity to retain and process that information any longer than 30 seconds. As he matures his attention span and ability to process information will expand in proportion to his age and quality of training.

Sometimes pup is just not going to perform at the same high level today as he did yesterday. This is not an indication of failure on his part or a reflection on poor training techniques. And it is not an uncommon problem. Be patient. Don't force him into exercises at this point. Perhaps pup is more concerned with the neighbor's cat today or he has picked up an exciting new scent that he wants to investigate. Or maybe he is just tired.

Whatever the reason, he just isn't clicking. In this respect, he is like you and me. We can't perform at 100 percent efficiency every day. So why should we expect pup to be any different? He will have his good days, bad days and those in between.

There may be another reason for his poor performance. Maybe, just maybe, it's you. Think about what and how you are communicating through your voice and body language. It might be that you are giving the right commands, but you are giving them on a different emotional and mental level. Review your day's events. Did you have a disagreement with your boss? An argument with your spouse or the kids? Another unusual event that might have affected your emotional or mental well-being? Before you get critical with pup, it might help to see how your voice and mannerisms are affecting him. Pup can and will quickly sense these emotional variables. The change will confuse him and produce a lackluster performance.

If you are upset, you and pup will be better served by postponing the training session and allowing pup to have a playtime. There is no justifiable reason for pup to become the target of your frustrations. It is far better to scrub the session and simply spend some time together. Pup needs playtime and this is an excellent occasion for it. He needs to check out the yard, explore new scents, get acquainted with the neighbors and just relax in your presence. You will, however, need to supervise and maintain discipline. Keep him out of danger spots such as busy streets and the neighbor's flower garden. Pup is much like a small child. He is curious about what goes on around him and that's healthy, up to a point. He does need your supervision to keep him out of harm's way.

As you prepare to train pup, keep an open mind about what you know about dogs. Many people have preconceived opinions about what should or should not be done in training and fail to consider new ideas. Make a practice of reading articles by other trainers, including bird-dog trainers. They are a valuable source of training information. Ask other owners how they resolved a particular problem. After gaining as much information as possible, apply that and what you already know about pup to the situation at hand. There are many folks who know a lot about dogs, but it is doubtful if anyone knows everything about dogs or even a particular dog. In other words, there are many experts. Use what you think applies to your situation along with your best judgment and common sense.

Pup will have his own unique personality. Again, he is comparable to a small child, energetic and willing to learn and please. But he lacks concentration and experience. Just as children are different and learn at various levels and in differing degrees, so it is with Beagle puppies. They vary in temperament, personality and ability to learn. The astute trainer, regardless of experience, learns something each time he trains a new puppy. This is partly because the trainer must discover the personality and ability of the individual puppy while training him to learn the basic skills, using patience, gentleness, consistency, simplicity, repetition and persistence. Sometimes there's a question who is really getting trained in the process, the student or the trainer.

Training pup is a challenge and adventure for both you and him. It is a cooperative effort. Your commitment and dedication allow pup to develop his potential hunting skills and become a useful partner in pursuing rabbits. His energy, enthusiasm, genetics and willingness to please and learn will help you focus on the positive aspects of the job. The rewards are extremely satisfying as you see pup progress in the development of his skills.

Chapter 5
Yard Training: The Basics

Most folks would probably agree that learning begins at birth and continues throughout life. So it is with pup. In a span of two to 16 weeks he has learned to respond to his mother, siblings, perhaps other pen mates, his original owner and you. Since you have acquired him, he has learned to adjust to a new environment consisting, at the very least, of new people, new scents and new voices.

So you are certain of one fact: pup can learn. Whether he has learned through mental processes, habit or pure instinct is subject to debate. Now he is about to embark upon a new adventure—learning in a routine, intense manner. Some of the routines will be easy and enjoyable. Others will be demanding. Nevertheless, all of it is necessary for pup to develop his potential as a hunter and companion. Just as no soldier should be expected to fight in combat without intense training neither can pup be expected to perform at his maximum potential without being taught basic skills.

The term "yard training" applies to the exercises of pup's basic training. This term is used because most of the exercises take place in the yard. However, training should occur wherever and whenever pup is in your presence.

In an earlier chapter, I talked about mealtimes being more than the provision of the basic necessities of food and water. It's an excellent opportunity to instill basic discipline and develop understanding between yourself and pup.

Formal yard training is intended to instill pup with basic disciplines necessary for you to exercise a measure of control over his actions. It can be described as pup's elementary education. Yard training provides pup the opportunity to learn verbal commands and become more accustomed to your voice, scent and mannerisms. It is preliminary to field training.

Length of Session

It may seem surprising, but the length of the yard-training session is a very important consideration. The session should never exceed one hour. Why only one hour? Why not go at it for as long as you feel like it? The answer: while pup can absorb a tremendous amount of information, he can only process that information in small amounts. His concentration and attention span are extremely short.

When sessions are pushed beyond the one-hour limit, pup begins to tire, becomes bored, distracted and difficult to manage. Depending upon pup's personality, you might even consider beginning with 15 or 20 minutes of exercises and spending the balance of the hour in playtime. Does this mean limiting the amount of time you spend together? Absolutely not! Spend as much time aspossible with him. Just limit the amount of time spent in actualexercises.

During yard training, pup will learn how to behave while on a leash and yard chain, how to enter the carrier box without hesitation, and how to behave while confined in the box. In addition, he will learn a series of verbal commands that will include the one negative command "No." The others are come, sit, down, up, stay and a combination command, sit-stay.

As pup learns these basic commands and exercises, it will be important for you to provide him additional opportunities to practice. Mealtimes and short trips in the carrier box while running errands are excellent opportunities for practice.

Yard training should be completed in approximately 20 hours for the average Beagle puppy. This can vary depending on pup's interest and ability to learn, combined with the skill, time available and dedication of the trainer. The 20-hour period is based on my experience. It is not a hard and fast rule. The number of hours is secondary to assuring that pup has his act together before he is taken afield.

Regardless of the time it takes to complete the yard-training exercises, pup will be exposed topossible failure and harm if you put him in the field without adequate preparation. It will also increase your frustration level trying to handle and control him in the field if you have cut his yard training short.

Praise and Rewards

It is the rare individual who does not appreciate the occasional compliment for accomplishing a difficult task. Those of us who are common working folks would most likely produce nothing if we were not rewarded with an occasional paycheck. And while praise or compliments are not absolutely necessary, they are certainly appreciated now and then. Children, without question, respond positively to praise and rewards. While pup is not human, he is very similar to a child. When praised and rewarded for accomplishing a task, he will not only display pleasure, but also will expect to be given attention each time. So praise him every time he accomplishes a task and reward him when he does so in a superior manner.

For some unknown reason, dogs in general and puppies in particular respond to the term, "That's." It seems they can somehow relate to the tone of the word, the voice in which it is given or the term itself. It seems odd, but when used, it shows in their next performance. For example, when you call pup to come to you and he races to meet you, praise him with the words, "That's a good pup." Use the term habitually whether in yard training or field work. Always give praise within 30 seconds of the completed action.

Rewards can be small treats, given when pup performs in an exceptional manner. Combined with praise, small treats can become powerful training tools. Plain, white bread, broken into small pieces, is a good choice, although anything pup enjoys eating will work just as well. Bread bits are convenient because they can be easily stored in a plastic bag and carried in your pocket during sessions. Again, it is important to remember to give the treat or reward, using the term, "That's a good pup," within 30 seconds of the completed action.

Protected Time

If there is a key rule for training, it would be a rule of privacy. Call it protected time, privacy hour or anything you choose. The important thing is that the time you set aside for yard training is time for you and pup. Closed practice is vital so you and pup can use the time to develop communication and companionship. It's difficult enough to train without the added distractions of casual observers. Some distractions will be unavoidable, such as the neighbor's cat, traffic noises, etc. Casual observers add to the problem. Pup loves to play and the presence of others will distract him from his primary business and tempt him to seek the attention and affection of anyone else present.

Insofar as possible, eliminate as many distractions as you can. If you own other dogs, keep them penned or chained. If small children are around, try to keep them out of pup's line of sight. Because pup is untrained and undisciplined, he will be tempted to play and chase them. When this happens, it's best to cancel the session.

How do you deal with unexpected company that happens to arrive during a training session? Simply cancel the session. Pup isn't going to learn much anyway. This doesn't mean to hide pup away somewhere. It's perfectly acceptable to keep him near you when you are in the presence of others. Again, simply cancel the exercises for the day and pick up where you left off at the next session. Your unexpected company won't know the difference.

The only exception to the protected-time rule is if you have a family member or hunting partner who is vitally interested in assisting you in training pup. If no such person is available, keep the closed-practice rule in force for at least the first 10 hours. Eventually, pup will benefit greatly from the company of others but for now it's best to keep things between you and him.

The Leash

One of your first actions after acquiring pup was fitting him with a plain collar. By this time, he has become accustomed to having something around his neck. Now it is time for him to learn to respond to following you on a leash. In fact, leash training can begin at the time the collar goes around his neck. The rule is the sooner the better. Whether the leash is chain, nylon or rope is of minor consequence. However, the advantage of a chain leash is that it discourages pup from excessive chewing during training sessions.

Use of the O-ring on the collar is optional and can be disregarded during training. Slip the leash around his neck and fasten it onto the chain with the snap in a loop fashion, so he can feel the pressure being applied when you ask him to go with you.

Some might question the practice of placing a loop of any kind around a puppy's neck for fear of choking or injury. But there are benefits. If pup starts to struggle and fight the leash, don't exert pressure. Stoop, squat or kneel down and reassure him with your voice and hands. He will quickly quiet down. Do this repeatedly, and praise him each time he quiets down. Pup will quickly learn that the leash is not to be feared. When he feels the gentle tightening of the leash on his neck, he will be more inclined to follow your bidding. He will associate the pressure caused by the leash with the leash itself, not you. This is an important consideration. You are not trying to train pup to fear you. You just want him to respond appropriately to your commands and requests.

Leash-training exercises should be performed at least once a day for a duration of two or three minutes, for as many days as necessary for him to become accustomed to the leash. It is recommended these exercises be

When pup is on a leash, don't exert pressure if he becomes excited.

performed inside the pen for the first three to five days or until he follows willingly for short distances.

After he has become comfortable being led inside the pen, pup is ready for outside sessions. His first mistake will probably be to bolt ahead, coming to an abrupt halt when he reaches the end of the leash. Use the no command to get his attention. Kneel down and gently reassure him with your voice and hands that all will be okay. Begin again. Take a couple of steps and allow him to find his range while leashed. Then gently coax him to follow you. Talk to him. Reassure him. Each time he responds appropriately, praise him. Give him plenty of encouragement. Pup wants to be with you. He just needs practice. Walk him for a minimum of five minutes. If he appears to be getting the hang of it, allow him more time. Lead him to the different corners of the yard. Let him stop frequently to sniff at objects and scents. Try to get him to relax. Make the exercise enjoyable for both of you.

Generally, puppies learn to follow on a leash fairly quickly if given enough practice. Leash training is important for the establishment of communication with pup and a necessity for his development and handling in the future. Imagine what it would be like trying to lead a non-leash trained dog out of the woods, through brush, thickets, swamps, fencerows and briar patches. It takes only one such experience to appreciate the benefits of thorough leash training.

Pup will learn quickly that the leash is his opportunity to be with you. After his third or fourth session, he will probably become excited when he sees the leash because he will know it's his opportunity to spend time with you.

Following Without the Leash

Training pup to follow you without the leash will require a measure of trust and judgment on your part. These non-leash exercises are designed to allow pup limited independence in your presence while learning to follow you with voice commands only. These exercises will pay large dividends when pup begins field training. His inherited stubbornness makes it impossible to guarantee that he will respond every time he is called, but these exercises will help condition him to respond appropriately most of the time.

If your yard is fenced, these exercises will be less complicated. Even

Use trust and judgment when training pup to follow without the leash.

so, you need to check for escape holes pup might be able to slip through. If your yard is open or unfenced, survey the area. Fix boundaries in your mind that you don't want pup to cross. Look for danger points such as yard edges bordered by busy streets, flower gardens, etc. Decide ahead of time what is off limits to pup and be prepared to enforce those boundaries by using the no command.

Place pup on the leash and lead him out of the pen. Keep him leashed while walking him for about five minutes. Then quietly slip the leash off his neck. Walk leisurely for five or six paces, saying "come, puppy, come." If he responds, praise him with the phrase, "That's a good puppy." If he bolts, sharply say "no," and quickly get the leash on him. Walk him leashed for another five minutes and repeat the off-leash exercise. Continue this routine until he follows you within a few paces for three or four minutes. Each session, expand the time but not the distance.

During these non-leash sessions, pup is bound to become distracted at some point and will attempt to cross one of your forbidden boundaries. When that happens, say "no" immediately. Stoop, squat or kneel down to his level and give the command come. If he ignores you, walk over to him and place him back on the leash. Walk him on-leash back to the

Give the Come command in a squatting position for best results.

spot where you gave the command. This action tells pup you want him to come to the point where you were. If he does respond when called, heap on the praise and give him a treat. This lets him know that he is responding appropriately and he will be rewarded.

If pup continually ignores your commands of no and come during these non-leash exercises, you will need to introduce him to the yard chain for control purposes.

The Yard Chain

The yard chain is a 10- to 12-foot chain with swivel snaps on both ends. It is usually available wherever pet supplies are sold and is used primarily for staking out a dog, allowing him maneuverability up to the length of the chain. While pup will need to remain quiet when staked out, the purpose for the chain in this session can best be described as an extended or long leash. Instead of using a regular leash, use the chain by snapping it to the 0-ring on his collar or by otherwise affixing it securely to the collar. The individual lengths in the chain make it difficult to loop it around his neck without extreme difficulty.

When the chain is in place, allow pup to reach a length of six or seven feet before gently applying pressure. This allows him to find his range. Begin walking slowly, bidding him to come. Allow him to stop frequently

The yard chain can be used to train pup to follow close.

to investigate scents and places. When you decide to proceed, give the command "come" and gently pull the chain. When he obeys your command, praise him lavishly. Gradually allow him more distance by feeding out the chain. After each stop, repeat the command "come, puppy," and praise him. When he approaches a forbidden border, say, "no" or "no, puppy." If he refuses to stop, apply pressure on the chain by pulling on it gently. This action will stop him. At the same time, repeat the command "no" or "no, puppy." When he comes to a complete stop, say, "That's a good puppy." Stoop, squat or kneel down and give him the command come. Now, when he comes, praise him again and give him a treat.

In a short time, usually in two or three sessions, he will be ready to go without the chain. Remember that he learns by repetition. So if he needs more practice, continue these sessions until he responds to the no command when he arrives at a forbidden border and comes when called. Be sure to keep all commands short, simple and consistent. You will be surprised how quickly he will learn these particular exercises and begins following you without the chain or leash.

Verbal Commands

The Command "Come." The come command is undoubtedly the least difficult to teach of the verbal commands. Pup is conditioned to responding to you because you have established yourself as his primary provider. He looks to you for food, water, general care and companionship. These factors greatly affect his behavior. Training of this command begins almost immediately after he has been placed in his new surroundings.

Being a puppy, he is curious and wants to please. He also wants and enjoys attention, especially petting and praise. Training for the verbal command come and most other commands plays upon these facets of his personality. The key training factors to remember are patience, simplicity and repetition.

Another important element is being able to relate to pup on his own level. To accomplish this, try to see his world as he physically views things. Pup is small. At full growth, his head and eyes will rarely extend 24 inches above the ground. So it's important to remember his perspective of the world is quite different from yours. He has a fabulous sense of smell. Some estimates suggest it is 700 times more powerful than that of the average human being. His sense of smell is one of his major assets. On the other hand, he is color blind and does not identify colors. Instead, he views objects in various shades of gray. What does this tell you as pup's

The No command should be given with arm shoulder high, palm of hand out.

handler and trainer? Basically, it suggests that if you remain motionless, there is a chance that he won't see you. So your movements are very important. When you move, it helps pup focus his attention on you. If you give the command come while standing perfectly still, pup might respond because he is attuned to your voice. But to ensure that pup is really paying attention, give the command first while standing; then squat or kneel, move your hand slightly and give the command again. While you are in the lowered position, it's a good bet that he will respond more quickly and enthusiastically. You have provided him an opportunity to respond while using all of his senses on his level. Your movement helps him to locate your position. When he comes on your command, lavish him with praise, petting and treats (optional). Usually, he will respond without treats but if his personality is recalcitrant, treats can make a difference.

Use the command come frequently during training. Use it while he is on a leash or yard chain, during playtimes and at every opportunity. Remember, he learns through repetition. It may become tedious and boring for you but it won't be for him.

When you stoop, squat, or kneel and give the come command, pup will probably respond by running to you, nearly knocking you over on his arrival. That's exactly what you want initially. He will eventually learn through practice and other exercises to temper his enthusiasm. What's important is getting him accustomed to responding to your requests to come when called. By training him to come when called, you have established a confidence builder for both of you. He has learned to please you with his response and you have taught him the first command. If both of you can accomplish this first step, it will give you the confidence to proceed with the other exercises. Keep in mind that pup can be very, very stubborn. It's not totally his fault. It's part of his heredity. And that same stubbornness will become an important positive factor in hunting. Nevertheless, he must learn to respond to your call. Persistence, patience and practice will be necessary. So don't get discouraged if he ignores your commands in the early stages of training. Just continue providing him practice opportunities. He will eventually respond on command.

The Negative Command "No" and the Reasons for it. Dog training is generally considered a positive, upbeat activity. Words and phrases such as playtime, praise, rewards, treats, dog and master, companionship, development of communication, relationship enhancement, petting and the like are all positive notions that dominate the endeavor. However, pup will need to learn at least one command that will protect him and allow you some control over his actions.

Undoubtedly, you and pup have already shared some interesting experiences and not a few heated conversations. The interesting experiences probably include actions on pup's part such as bolting out of the pen when you inadvertently neglected to close the gate. He has probably jumped on you after stepping in some unpleasantly odorous substance. He has probably turned over his food or water bowl, barked at neighbors, phantoms in the night and free-running dogs in the wee hours of the morning. As for the conversations, they probably range from unprintable epithets to pleas for cooperation involving the aforementioned interesting experiences.

Unfortunately, some of you erroneously believe you have to tolerate such behavior. You mistakenly think that misbehavior goes with dog ownership and the puppy will eventually outgrow the pattern. Perhaps he will, but what if he doesn't? The result is a seriously flawed dog through no fault of his own.

So if pup is creating havoc, you need to take corrective action. The lack of communication between you and pup can be corrected by using a short, simple command to let pup know of your disapproval. It must be administered quickly (remember the 30-second rule), consistently and firmly. That command is the word "No."

— 67 —

The training of the command no is a critical element in pup's discipline and, as you shall see, his safety. Remember, there is absolutely no place in pup's training for corporal punishment. In fact, if you strike him, you will effectively lose his confidence and will only create more training problems. Teaching him the proper response to the command no will prevent such problems. The key to training this command is to give it in a firm, sharp tone of voice. Pup will immediately detect this tone change when you first use it. This is to your advantage because, for a few seconds at least, you will have his undivided attention.

I have always had an aversion to neighbors who allow their dogs to bark incessantly at all hours of the day or night. And I will not allow any dog in my possession to bark constantly, thus jeopardizing the tranquillity of the neighborhood. Also, many cities have laws that can result in fines and court costs for negligent dog owners. I prefer to spend my money differently.

The earlier pup understands the no command the better. If, for example, he begins to bark when you leave the pen area after feeding him, turn quickly, raise your arm with your palm out as though you were giving a stop sign, point at him and say sharply (shout if you must) "No!!!" If pup continues to bark, give the command again. Continue to give the command for as many times as is necessary until he ceases barking. Young puppies will usually respond fairly quickly. When he ceases barking, praise him in a complimentary voice by saying, "That's a good pup." Remember, you must give the command each time he barks, even if it means getting out of bed in the middle of the night.

For a dog with serious barking or other behavior problems, use a rolled-up newspaper and slap it against your hand or thigh, immediately after voicing the command. With enough repetition, even the most serious barkers can be cured over time.

Most assuredly, there are times when pup should be allowed to bark, such as when there are prowlers (human or animal) violating his territory or when his security is threatened for one reason or another. But these instances should be the exception rather than the rule. Remember, it is the responsibility of the owner/trainer to control a dog's behavior, ethically if not legally. Using the no command can help accomplish this task.

Aside from controlling incessant barking, no can be a safeguard for pup in the yard and in the field. The following examples may help clarify the point:

My wife and I own (who truly owns a cat?) a Siamese cat that considers the house and the yard her domain. Over the years, Smokey has dominated the neighborhood as Queen Cat. Her attitude toward dogs is toleration toward some and total disdain for most. For instance, she and my female Beagle, Bell, got along splendidly. But her relationship with the male, Sam, was antagonistic. She would have scratched his eyes out if given the opportunity. During the hot summer months, I routinely put both dogs on yard chains while cleaning the pen. On one occasion, I noticed Smokey playing with Bell. A few minutes later, I glanced at Sam and realized quickly that he was not pleased with the cat intruding on what he considered to be his territory. He was straining at the end of the chain, hair on his back bristling. Smokey was poised to spring at him. I knew instantly I couldn't do anything to control the actions of the cat, so I quickly shouted, "Sam, no." He immediately turned his head to face me, relaxed and backed away. His response to the command no very likely saved him from some nasty cat-claw lacerations, and it probably saved me from an unnecessary vet bill. So, the no command is handy around the yard and in the general handling of pup.

The second situation happened in the field and involved my female Beagle, Bell. The incident took place while rabbit hunting on a friend's property a few miles from my home. The farm is bordered on the east side by a large drainage ditch that flows roughly north and south. The fields on the west side of the ditch are traditionally planted in rice or soybeans. It was late fall and the rice crop had been harvested. Rabbits found cover on the ditch banks so it was likely one of the dogs would strike a scent line in that area. I was walking on the edge of the field allowing the dogs to work the brush and heavy cover. As we started south, I noticed that Bell was air scenting while moving cautiously through a briar patch. Suddenly she stopped. I saw what looked like a black stick, moving in a circular motion. At first I couldn't identify the odd-looking item, so I walked up to get a better look. Then I saw the white stripe—a skunk poised to defend itself. I shouted, "Bell, No!" She froze in her tracks. I then gave the command to come and she responded immediately. She did receive a small tainting of the awful spray, but she escaped a major dosing. In addition, several rabid skunks had been killed in this locale during the late summer and early fall. A disaster may have been prevented because Bell had been thoroughly trained to respond to the no command.

There have been numerous other times over the years when the command has helped avert danger. It is important to remember to give the command in a firm authoritative voice. If the command is given in a mild, weak voice, pup will simply continue doing whatever he was doing before the command was given. In other words, he will ignore the command. Give the command within 30 seconds of pup's action. Otherwise, it will be ineffective. Again, especially during yard training, follow the corrected action with verbal praise. Be consistent. Give the command every time you want pup to stop whatever he is doing.

Once you begin using the command no, don't change it to stop, halt, or anything else under any circumstances. Once pup understands no, other words simply become noise to him.

Other uses for the no command: training pup not to jump on you or on other people, training him to remain inside the pen even when the gate is open, or training him to stop when he bolts and attempts to run away. It will take many repetitions before pup's response becomes a developed habit. But be patient, consistent and persistent. The more practice (and maturity) pup gets the more proficient he will become at obeying the command.

The Command "Sit." The "sit" command is not as difficult to teach as you might expect. It is slightly more complex because it requires physical guidance and voice command simultaneously. As a practical matter, it should be initiated inside the pen at meal time. The advantage of training at meal time is that the feed is a convenient treat or reward.

Begin by squatting or stooping so you are on pup's level. Place your right hand back where his back leg joints meet his spine or hindquarters. (If you are left-handed, reverse the hand positions.) Gently lift your left hand, placing gentle pressure upward on his jaw and simultaneously push down gently with your right hand. While doing this, say, "sit" or "sit, puppy." When he is in the sitting position, praise him by saying, "That's a good puppy." Repeat the exercise three or four times for a minimum of five days. By then, pup should be getting the idea that if he sits when asked, he will be rewarded. His food will be given to him as a matter of course whether or not he obeys. Nevertheless, pup will begin to sense that the command sit has edible rewards.

At first, pup will be very excited and wiggly. Don't expect him to sit for more than a second or two. That's okay. Give him plenty of praise. Try to add one second for each exercise. Eventually, with practice and patience, he will learn to sit until you give him another command to move.

If pup is a slow learner, be patient and persistent. Continue with the hands-on exercises until he responds correctly. After a while you will be able to give the sit command and he will respond immediately. Reward him within 30 seconds with an extra treat such as bread bits or a small piece of meat placed in his bowl. Lavish praise on him. Make a big deal over his accomplishment. He needs to know you are pleased with him when he performs as you command.

The sit command can and should be used as a matter of course on a

The Sit command is not as difficult as some might expect.

daily basis. After pup has learned the correct response, give the command as you enter the pen. This will help eliminate the annoying habit of pup jumping up on you. You can use the command in conjunction with the no command by saying, "No, puppy, sit." Both commands are short and generally cause no confusion. Remember to praise him. Pet him and give him treats if they are readily available. Within 10 to 15 days pup should be responding appropriately. Thereafter, treats can be eliminated; only praise and petting will be needed.

When you have pup on the leash, stop occasionally and give the command sit. If he fails to respond, gently lift up on the leash and press down on his hindquarters. Have him remain in the sitting position until you give the command come accompanied by a gentle pull of the leash. Repeat this exercise six to eight times each session. Again, use praise, petting and treats to reward correct action.

The Commands "Stay" and "Sit-Stay." When pup is proficient on the command sit, it's time to begin the command "stay." This command is extremely useful when you need pup to remain still while you perform some minor chore. For example, you may need to open a padlock with a key, an activity that usually requires the use of both hands. Pup has already learned the sit command, so all you need to do is give that command and he will either sit or lie quietly while you attend to the chore. Pup should be on a leash in the initial stages of training for the stay command. This exercise will require ample amounts of patience, persistence, consistency and a measure of trust on your part. But the results are certainly worth the effort. The sit-stay command should become a regular routine exercise.

As a practical matter, begin the stay command while pup is in the pen or kennel and you have him in the sit position. Once he is in the sit position (even if you must physically guide him into it) and you are in a

Sit-Stay should begin inside the pen or kennel.

stooping or squatting position, give the command to stay. Rise slowly to your feet and raise your arm, extending it toward him, palm flattened and say, "Stay, puppy." When he begins to fidget and move, give the command no. While you have his attention, say, "Sit, stay, puppy." Follow this routine for as many repetitions as necessary until he is able to remain in the sit-stay position for at least two seconds. Count the seconds—one-thousand one...one-thousand-two, etc. Practice this command daily (feed time is excellent), adding two seconds for each session. When pup performs as you command, be sure to reward him with praise and treats. After about a week of these daily exercises, pup should begin to show progress.

When training the sit-stay command outside the pen, you will inevitably encounter distractions. Remember that pup's attention span is still very short and he is curious about his surroundings. To neutralize the distractions and provide some control over his actions while training this command, place him on the yard chain. Begin by walking him as though he were on a regular leash. Stop frequently and let him practice the commands come and sit. After 5-10 minutes, or whenever he appears comfortable, gradually allow him additional slack or distance, perhaps six to eight feet from you. Stop walking for brief moments and give the command sit-stay. Hold the yard chain perfectly still. When he looks at you, raise your hand about shoulder height, palm flat and facing him, and continue repeating the command. If he moves, say, "No, stay." If he remains motionless for at least three seconds, kneel or squat and call him to you. When he responds, immediately heap on the praise. Give lots of petting and reward him with a treat. Repeat the exercise five or six times on the first day, expanding the required time for him to remain in the stay or sit-stay position by two seconds for each exercise.

On following days or sessions, lengthen the amount of yard chain and the number of seconds you want him to remain in position. Do this until you have extended the chain all the way. By this time, pup is getting used to the exercise and is enjoying the treats. Now it's time to begin extending the distance even more between you and pup. Begin routinely, as though it's going to be a regular exercise on the yard chain. But this time, when you stop him and have him in the sit-stay position, lay the chain on the ground. Very slowly, back away from the chain, repeating, "sit- stay" with your hand in the air, palm out and facing him. If he begins to move, sharply give the command, "No, sit-stay." After moving slowly backwards for six to eight steps, call him to you. When he responds, rewards are again in order. As you repeat the exercise, add two or three steps and simultaneously add one or two seconds. If, at any point, pup moves from his original position, repeat the exercise until he has accomplished the individual step of time and distance. As he accomplishes each step, continue to add distance (steps) and time (seconds). Pup can only learn the exercise through repetition.

After six to eight sessions, pup should be ready for the next phase—obeying the sit-stay command while you walk away from him and remain out of sight.

Begin routinely because pup now understands the sit-stay exercise. This time, when you place the chain on the ground, turn around and begin walking away from him. At first, he will probably attempt to follow you. When this happens, turn quickly to face him and give the command, "No, stay!" Repeat this exercise until you can walk at least 10-12 steps without him following. Then say, "That's a good puppy, come." Give plenty of praise, petting and rewards. As you repeat the exercise, add time and distance. Remember, pup is still wearing the chain and is dragging it as he comes to you. He is in no particular danger, provided you have removed any obstacles the chain might catch on.

As you continue to extend the time and distance, find a location where you can be out of pup's sight but allows you to see him. This could be a large tree, the corner of a garage or house, or any place where your view of pup is unobstructed but he cannot see you. When pup has advanced in his discipline to remain in the stay position for at least 30 seconds while you are in sight, without use of the no command, you will want him to remain in the stay position until called, when he can't see you but can hear your voice. If your yard or training area does not have a natural obstruction, you can use a large cardboard box. Get pup in the sit-stay position. Lay the chain on the ground and place the box in a position between you and him so he can't see you.

Using either the box or a natural obstruction, give the command to sit-stay and slowly walk away. The distance can be up to 50 or 60 feet. But the distance isn't as important as the opportunity for you to hide from him, yet keeping him in sight. Remain very quiet while pup stays in his designated position. Keep him in suspense for approximately 10 seconds. If he remains in position, call him to you. When he responds, heap on the praise and rewards. If pup moves, reposition him, giving the command, "No, sit-stay," and repeat the exercise. Be sure to reposition him at the original place. Gradually, expand the time and distance. After six to eight exercises, pup will begin to remain in the stay position until he hears you call him.

A cardboard box can hide you from pup. Yes, there is really a Beagle behind it!

When pup has learned to remain in the stay position for 20 seconds and responds correctly to all your commands, slip the yard chain off him and replace it with a regular leash. Begin the exercise exactly as you have been practicing with the chain. By now, pup has learned that to obey your commands brings rewards. While walking him on the leash, stop frequently and give the command stay and drop the leash on the ground. If he moves, say, "No, sit-stay." Require him to stay until you pick up the leash. A gentle tug on the leash or the command come will be his signal to move. Practice this exercise each time you get him out of the pen.

It's unreasonable to expect pup to remain in the stay position for more than 20-30 seconds while he is in yard training. Holding a longer stay comes with practice and maturity. Be consistent, firm, gentle, persistent and repetitious each time you want him to stay in one place. Eventually, he will stay until you tell him to move with a simple voice command. He just needs a lot of practice.

The Command "Up." There are two reasons for teaching pup the "up" command. First, pup is going to be transported in a vehicle, requiring him either to climb onto a seat and into a carrier or to jump onto the bed of a pickup truck with the tailgate lowered. Second, he will inevitably encounter wire-mesh fences while field training and rabbit hunting. Rabbits are notorious for living in fence-row areas and are masters at weaving in and out of the mesh wire to escape varmints and dogs. So training pup the up command is an important step for both hunting and transporting situations. Most dogs eventually learn to handle these situations through trial and error, but it's certainly advantageous for both you and pup to master the routine before beginning field work.

I will first discuss the up command used principally in yard training. The field training up command will be detailed in a later chapter.

You will need some props for proper training of this routine: a leash, three or four feet of stairs and a platform. If you are fortunate to have a set of stairs and porch, you are ready to start. If not, you can easily

The Up command teaches pup to jump onto the bed of a pickup truck.

construct a few steps out of scrap lumber. Scrap lumber is suggested because once pup has learned the initial command, there will be little use for the contraption, unless you wish to keep it for training additional puppies. If you own a pickup truck, you can place the stairs up to the lowered tail gate and use the truck bed as a platform.

For the sake of this discussion, I assume you have a set of stairs elevating to a porch floor three or four feet off the ground. Begin this exercise with pup on a leash. Lead him to the stairs and encourage him to climb the first step by gently pulling the leash straight up, simultaneously giving the command, "Up, puppy." Continue until he is able to place his front feet up on the first step. Now pup is standing with his front feet on the step and his back feet on the ground. Continue to encourage him and command, "Up, puppy." If he suddenly pulls backwards and begins to fight the leash, kneel and gently calm him with your hands and voice. Then begin again. If after four attempts he has not pushed up with his back legs to gain the first step, stoop down again and place your hand below his tail and above his hocks. Gently lift him up onto the step. Give him praise and a reward. Place him back on the ground and begin again. Repeat this exercise for 8-10 minutes. Each time he manages to gain the first step with your help, give praise and rewards.

Now get him on the ground and give the up command, leading with the leash but using no other physical assistance. Unless pup is a very slow learner, he should be attempting to get up the step or steps. However, if he still needs physical assistance, provide it until he no longer needs the help, other than the leash pressure. Remember to reward him each time he climbs or jumps up a step. Each session, add another step until he can master all the steps to the platform. It's entirely possible that pup will scramble up to the top step and platform on the very first day, but in case he is the reluctant type, add a step each session. Reward him as he progresses using the following sequences: He masters the first step on the first day; all is well and fine; the next session he masters step one and two; reward him for step two but not step one. The next session he masters step three. Reward him for step three but not one and two, etc. Using this routine, even the most timid puppy should be scrambling to the top of the stairs by the fourth or fifth session.

The next process will require pup to reach the second step without the benefit of the first, a variation of skipping stairs. This can easily be accomplished by blocking off the first step with a cardboard box or pieces of lumber tied together. Any obstacle can be used so long as it blocks the first step but allows pup to place his front paws on the second step.

Stairs can be blocked off to help teach the Up command.

Give the up command and place gentle pressure on the leash, lifting straight up. Pup might need some physical help at first. When he is on the second step, either on his own or with your help, double the amount of the reward.

Begin again with pup on the ground and repeat the exercise until he can master the second step easily. Continue these sequences until he can obtain the platform without any assistance except the leash pressure. Throughout these exercises, consider his size. Don't ask him to do something he is physically incapable of doing. Gradually eliminate steps as he grows. Once he has learned to push with his back legs, he should be able to jump onto a three-foot-high platform at about 21 weeks. The up exercise should become a routine part of his training sessions.

The Command "Down." Once pup has experienced getting up the stairs and onto the platform, he next needs to learn how to get down without assistance. It is important to remember that excessive lifting of the puppy, either up or down, will foster an unnecessary dependency upon you as the trainer. So the rule is don't lift him up or down unless absolutely necessary. His size will be the determining factor.

Start the "down" command after pup reaches the first step. Placing gentle pressure on the leash, give the command, "Down, puppy." Most likely he will have no problem getting to the ground. Give praise and rewards when he completes the task. Continue to move him up and down the first step for six to eight repetitions. Generally, pup will follow the leash as he has been trained and few problems will be encountered. By the time he is reaching the top stair or platform, he will be conditioned to follow with little or no hesitation. The problem arises when pup is asked to get down without the benefit of the stairs or steps.

Pup has a natural fear of heights, and it will be necessary for him to overcome this fear to learn jumping down to the ground. Judgment on your part will be important so pup doesn't inadvertently injure himself. Unnecessary injuries frequently occur to puppies because trainers require them to do things they are physically incapable of doing. Jumping off platforms that are beyond his physical capabilities is an example. That is the reason for teaching pup to descend the stairs or steps one at a time. As he grows, he can be expected to jump off a three or four-foot platform by the time he is four to five months old.

The up and down commands are usually learned gradually over time. Providing pup with the opportunity to learn them is most important. Be patient, consistent and repetitious. He will eventually be jumping up to the platform with ease and then to the ground without hesitation.

Use judgment when teaching the Down command.

The Carrier Box

The fiberglass animal transport/carrier box is a marvelous invention for transporting pup safely (see Chapter 3). It is also a valuable training tool. It is very light, durable, and can be moved conveniently. The box can also be used to confine pup while cleaning or performing routine repairs on his pen.

When pup is being box trained, at least two specific behaviors will be expected of him. One is to enter the box without hesitation, and the second is for him to remain quiet for the duration of his confinement. Experience shows most puppies prefer exactly the opposite—to hesitate or refuse to enter the box, and, once inside, to whine or bark constantly whether the box is stationary or in transit. This routine is designed to ensure quick, efficient entry and to reduce and eliminate the whining and barking.

Begin this exercise with pup on the leash. Set the box in an unobstructed area. Lead him to the box and allow him to investigate it by sniffing around it for a few minutes. While he is investigating, talk to him in a reassuring tone of voice. This will help him dispel any distrust or fears. Quietly open the gate so he can check out the entrance. If he chooses to go in, great. But don't expect him to enter automatically. This is new territory for him. He is unsure of himself. After four or five minutes of investigating, give the command, "In, puppy," and place gentle pressure on the leash, leading him toward the entrance. When he balks, place your free hand on his hindquarters and gently push him toward the open gate. Keep talking to him in a reassuring tone. If he balks on the second attempt, stop the exercise and walk him on the leash for approximately two minutes.

Lead him over to the box again. This time have a reward ready. Give the command, "In, puppy." Again, use gentle pressure on the leash and his hindquarters. When he is completely inside, give him the treat and pour on the praise and plenty of petting. Repeat this exercise at least four times the first session and increase it by one repetition each session for five days.

By now, pup should be going into the box because he expects a treat. The next step is to close the gate and isolate him from you. When pup has entered by correctly responding to the in command, give him a treat, reward him with praise and close the gate. Most likely he will just sit or lie down. Few puppies tend to fight to get out of the box once confined inside. Because the box has a grated front gate and ventilated sides, pup can see you. He is okay so long as you are in view. The problem begins

Pup needs to learn to enter the carrier box efficiently.

when he can't see you. This usually produces the whining and barking. To correct this misbehavior, you will need two props, a rolled-up newspaper and a canvas or blanket large enough to cover the box completely.

Begin the exercise exactly as described above. Once pup is inside and has received his reward, close the gate, cover the box with the canvas and step away about two steps. Stay within reach of the box but remain very quiet. Pup will probably remain silent for the first minute or so. But being isolated in a dark place away from you, he will begin to get a little nervous. When he begins to whine, give a sharp no command, by saying, "No, puppy. Be quiet!" If he responds by being quiet, lift the canvas, open the gate and give him a treat. Repeat this exercise four or five times the first session. On succeeding sessions, when pup is inside the box, remain quiet for as long as pup remains quiet. Extend your distance from the box a few steps. Each time he begins to whine or bark, give the command, "No, puppy, quiet!" If he ignores the command, immediately go to the box and hit the top of the box with the rolled-up newspaper, give the command again and back away.

Pup should be increasing the length of time he remains quiet with

It's important that pup learns to keep quiet while in the carrier box.

each exercise. If he can remain quiet without a command for an additional 30 seconds each session, reward him with treats upon his release from the box.

This exercise should be practiced during each training session. Unless pup is a very slow learner, by the time his yard training is completed, you should expect him to enter the box on command and remain quiet until released. Box training can also be practiced each time you clean or repair the pen.

But what to do if pup violates his discipline while being transported? This requires immediate corrective action: Stop your vehicle, go to the box (covered or uncovered) with a rolled-up newspaper (or your hand if a newspaper is not available), hit the top of the box and sharply give the command, "No, puppy, quiet!" After one or two instances, pup will learn that he can't misbehave in the box whether it is stationary or in transit. Again, it's up to you to administer the discipline within 30 seconds. If pup learns he can bark, whine and howl during transit, you will have a continuous problem. It is imperative that you take immediate action. Doing so prevents future problems for you and pup.

It is critical that discipline be maintained during all phases of pup's training. The only exception is during playtimes. And even then, be sure to keep him out of harm's way. Remember that yard training is designed to instill discipline and provide pup with the prerequisite skills to become a hunting companion. It also provides both you and pup time to become better acquainted and learn to work as a team.

Go slow with the training exercises. Keep your expectations reasonable. For example, pup can't be expected to jump onto the back of a pickup truck until he has grown large enough to accomplish such a feat. You may have to lift him to the bed of the truck for a while. But almost immediately, he can learn to come when called, respond to no, sit and stay, and follow on a leash. Use common sense and good judgment while training him for off-leash and yard-chain activities so as not to endanger him. Spend as much time as possible together but limit the exercises to not more than one hour per session. Allow ample playtimes so he can simply enjoy being with you and reduce stress. After about 20 hours of yard training you will be amazed at the skills he has learned and the knowledge and enjoyment you have gained. And remember, the things pup learns during these sessions will stay with him for many years.

Chapter 6
Field Training Preparations

Before loading pup in the carrier and heading for the field, ask yourself the following questions as a guide for preparations:

1. If you are a non-landowner, where will you train?
2. What are the primary training seasons?
3. Are you physically ready for the rigors of field training?
4. What type of clothing and props will you need?
5. What special items do you need?
6. What safety factors should be considered?
7. Is pup ready for the field?

Locating Training Areas

If you own land with a good crop of rabbits or have immediate access to a good training area, you are indeed fortunate. However, the vast majority of suburban residents don't own this kind of property. If pup is registered and you belong to a local Beagle club or similar organization, locating a training area is usually very simple. Many of these organizations lease or own training grounds especially designed for puppies. If you are not affiliated with an organization, the problem is slightly more complicated but not impossible to solve.

Potential public lands available for training can be located by contacting your local wildlife officer or state fish and game department. Often overlooked sources of public land are the Army Corps of Engineers, state or local forestry agencies, the federal Fish and Wildlife Service and military installations. All of these sources may provide information on land tracts that can be used by the public. Be sure to request a copy of any special regulations, particularly those pertaining to dog training. These public lands are usually accessible without fees, but be sure to inquire. If these resources are not available in your area and personal contacts through friends and acquaintances prove futile, personal reconnaissance may be your only available avenue.

Personal reconnaissance requires some time, effort and travel, but the results can be rewarding. The routine involves traveling the backroads of your community, beginning at the outer edges of the city limits. Most of the best areas are located off the main highways, so be sure to cover those out-of-the-way spots located on gravel and dirt roads. Look for areas that appear to harbor rabbits, such as covered fencerows, farm lanes, woods, woodlots, ditch banks, row crops, river bottoms, swamps, and lake and pond edges. When you have located a prospective area, you will need to seek out the owner and secure permission.

Securing permission to train on private land is very similar to acquiring permission to hunt. Although you won't be hunting, per se, at least initially the same courtesies and ethics one follows in hunting apply. Never assume you have permission to enter someone's land. Get the land owner's permission to enter his property.

Always get the landowner's permission to enter his property.

It is entirely possible, you will find no one at home when you stop to inquire because many landowners are employed at full-time jobs or their farming operations require their attention away from their homes. If this is the case, check for the name on the mailbox and/or go to the nearest neighbor. Introduce yourself and request the landowner's name and how he can be contacted. Always explain why you need to contact him. Often while inquiring with a neighbor, the neighbor will allow you permission to use his property as well.

When communicating with landowners, be specific about your intentions. Explain that your primary objective is to train pup to find and run (chase) rabbits. At the same time, ask him if he allows hunting because eventually pup will need to handle gun noise. If the owner objects to shooting, respect his wishes. Your immediate goal is to get an area where you can get pup into a field-training situation. Rabbit hunting areas can be located elsewhere at a later time.

Be sure to ask the landowner about any and all restrictions or rules. For example, part of his land may be under cultivation or used exclusively for livestock and he wants this section left undisturbed or avoided. Ask him about boundaries or property lines so you won't inadvertently trespass on his neighbors. You will also need to know where major roads or highways are located so you can avoid putting pup into a hazardous situation. Usually a rabbit will not cross a busy highway, but pup might get excited and inadvertently attempt to cross.

Landowners are extraordinarily cautious and suspicious of most strangers because of the rise in rural vandalism and theft. They are folks much like yourself. They want to know who you are and what you will be doing on their property. Be open, honest, courteous and tactful, even if the owner denies permission. He doesn't necessarily have to provide you with an explanation if he refuses to let you use his property.

If permission is granted, express your appreciation. Remember, you are an invited guest. When you leave his property, let him know. If no one is home, leave a thank-you note.

Special remembrances at Christmas, a telephone call and a thank-you note through the mail are excellent ways to foster good relationships with landowners. The key is to be thoughtful and courteous. It pays huge dividends. How you conduct yourself on other's property often opens or closes the door to other privately owned areas.

Locating and securing training/hunting areas on private lands is an on-going process. Why? Because land ownership changes hands. Urban sprawl and development eliminate large chunks of rabbit habitat. Rabbit populations tend to fluctuate from year to year. Areas that hold high populations one year may be nearly void of rabbits the next year. So be prepared to secure permission for several tracts of private land.

The Primary Training Seasons

The primary field training season may vary depending upon locale, but in the mid-south these are basically late fall, winter and early spring.

Late spring, summer and early fall in this region can be extremely uncomfortable to both dog and trainer because of heat and humidity. Pup doesn't sweat. He pants. His ability to dispense heat from his body is limited to his intake of water. Lack of water intake can lead to heat exhaustion, which can be a major problem.

Many hound owners opt for running their dogs at night, and some Beagle owners who run their dogs year around use this tactic. As a personal preference, I choose not to run or work dogs in the field during these seasons. It's tough on both trainers and dogs. If pup is properly trained, he will lose none of his learned abilities while sitting out these hot-weather seasons. Basic yard training can be conducted during this off season to keep him disciplined and sharp.

Other problems caused by late spring and summer field work include avoiding poisonous snakes and battling annoying insects such as mosquitoes, ticks, chiggers and biting flies. Little is gained by exposing yourself and pup to these aggravations and possible dangers.

During the primary training seasons of late fall, early spring and winter, be aware of weather patterns and changes. High winds can cause serious problems because pup can't hear you and you can't hear him. When the wind blows at 20-25 miles per hour, it is difficult to hear pup bark on a scent line or see him as he works the brush. Never let pup get out of range of your hearing at anytime for any reason. High winds just add to training frustrations and increase the risk of losing pup.

Early spring has its hazards, such as sudden thunderstorms. If you are caught in an open field you risk being struck by lightning. So take the necessary precautions. Rain, especially blowing rain, reduces your ability to hear pup.

Field training is a very positive endeavor, but the trainer needs to weigh each weather danger and make his best decision. Personally, I prefer not to field-train or run dogs during these extreme weather conditions and the seasons of late spring and summer. When nighttime temperatures begin to drop into the 50s, allowing heat to dissipate from the ground quickly, I'm ready to get into the field as soon as possible.

Being Physically Ready

As a field trainer, you don't need to be a fine-tuned Olympic athlete to withstand the demands of field training, but even if your health is generally good, you need to be aware of your limitations. Field training requires tough walking through brush, mud, snow, swamps, and hills, and across ditches and fences. If you are a desk jockey and spend a significant portion of your day sitting, common sense dictates you should prepare your legs and lungs for field-training sessions. This can be easily accomplished by increasing your walking each day.

If your daily routine requires considerable physical activity, you probably won't need additional conditioning. But that is a personal decision only you and/or your doctor can make. If you have a serious health problem, check with your doctor before undertaking field-training activities.

The toe-to-heel exercise prevents muscle pulls and cramps.

Because field training requires considerable walking, it's easy to strain or pull leg muscles. To reduce the risk, it's a good idea to do some leg-stretching exercises before getting pup out of the carrier. A very simple yet effective one is this: Place your hands against your truck or automobile about shoulder height and step backwards until you are standing on the front balls of your feet; slowly, push backwards on one leg until the heel of your foot touches the ground. Repeat the exercise with the other leg. After three to five repetitions, the tight leg muscles will loosen. This exercise will help reduce the risk of pulled muscles and reduce the possibility of painful leg cramps.

The physical requirements of field training probably fall in the range of moderate exercise. If you take your time, relax and are generally in good health, you should have few problems. Nevertheless, take precautions and use common sense.

The Right Clothing and Props

Weather generally dictates the type of clothing you will need for most field work. However, because you will be encountering briars, thorns, mud, water, ditches and fences, the right clothing will make field training a little easier.

Blue jeans are great for most outdoor activities but unless you can withstand thorn punctures and briar scratches in your hide, you will need something more substantial. A pair of "brush buster" hunting pants or a pair of leather or nylon chaps worn over jeans or trousers are an excellent investment. These pants and chaps last for years and will minimize wear and tear on both your legs and clothes.

A good pair of gloves is absolutely essential to ward off briars and thorns. And they protect against the elements as well. Indeed, gloves are so essential, you should carry an extra pair in your coat or pack in case one or both become lost.

Adequate, comfortable footwear is absolutely critical. Selection largely depends upon locale. Leather may be fine but if your hunting/training area contains swamps, marshes or water-filled ditches, waterproof footwear is preferable. Usually boots 10-12 inches high are sufficient. Be sure they are large enough for a pair of nylon and two pairs of heavy cotton socks (or if you prefer, one pair of nylon and one pair of heavy wool socks). Whether you choose leather or rubber boots, a handy way to store and transport them is in a large, paper grocery sack. The paper bag allows the boots to dry thoroughly and lasts a surprisingly long time. Developing the habit of putting on your boots when arriving at your area and removing them at the end of the day's field work prevents mud and debris from being tramped into your vehicle and, most importantly, into the house.

The head gear you choose should be comfortable and provide protection from the elements. A ski mask is a good choice for extremely cold

Proper clothing and props make field training a little easier.

days. It can be conveniently carried in a pack, coat pocket or possibles bag when not in use.

As an added safety precaution, always wear a blaze orange vest and head gear. They can prevent unfortunate accidents. During hunting trips, insist that other members of your party wear at least a blaze orange vest. You probably should be prepared to provide vests for those who do not have them. Several inexpensive ones can be stored conveniently behind the seat of a truck or elsewhere in a vehicle. All you need to do is hand it to the individual before the hunt begins.

Another handy prop is a long staff or walking stick. It need not be fancy. An old broom handle or length of sapling will usually fit the bill just fine. The staff is handy for several reasons. It will help you maintain your balance on uneven terrain and prevent falls. You are more likely to be injured by an accidental fall than being accidentally shot. The staff or stick can also be used to beat the bushes as you attempt to flush rabbits out of thick cover. In addition, pup gets used to seeing you carry something resembling a gun. When you begin to carry a gun instead of the stick, pup will already be conditioned to the idea.

Other Essential Items

Other items in the essential category include a good pocket knife and a poncho that can be placed in a plastic bag and stored in the game-bag section of your coat or vest. A "possibles bag" can be used for small items that are extremely useful in the field. The list may vary, but the following suggestions will help you get started: an extra leash or comparable length of rope, spare eyeglasses and eyeglass tool kit (if applicable), waterproof matches or lighter, paper or other tinder for emergency fire starting, small household candle, first aid items (bandaids, gauze, tape and antiseptic ointment, safety pins, extra gloves, a whistle for emergency signaling, miniature wrench/screwdriver set, spare bootlaces, compass, prescription medications, aspirin, antacid tablets and a current set of hunting regulations. All of these items can be placed inside a possibles bag and easily replaced after use. A used binocular case with a shoulder strap makes an excellent possibles bag.

Special Safety Considerations

An important common-sense action to take before heading out is to let someone know where you are going and approximately when you expect to return. Nothing upsets the marital applecart more quickly than not letting your spouse know where you intend to go and when you expect to return. For single folks, select your own contact person, but let someone know before you go traipsing off into the boondocks.

Finally, you might think the time has come to load pup in the carrier and head for the training area. Almost, but not quite. First, get a current copy of your state's hunting regulations and read them. Most sporting goods dealers provide them free of charge or at a very nominal fee. Make sure you find the section regarding dog-training and licensing requirements. Regulations vary from state-to-state, but a license is required even if you are only training and not hunting. Some states set dog-training seasons while others allow training or chase for pleasure year round with some restrictions. Read and know these rules as well as all trespass regulations. Some states require written permission from the land owner for you to enter private property; others do not. If you intend to train on public land, check the regulations for those areas. Just be sure you are familiar with the applicable regulations before going afield.

Is Pup Ready?

Most of your preparations have been completed. You have located an area suitable for training. The weather is suitable with night temperatures at least in the 50s. You have conditioned yourself into reasonably good physical shape. You have acquired the appropriate clothing and necessary props. You have assembled a possibles bag or pack and you are comfortable with it. You have considered the safety aspects of training alone. You have acquired the current hunting regulations, read them and have all the necessary licenses. Pup's vaccinations are up to date and he is in good physical condition.

Now is the time to ask: "How do I know pup is ready for field work?" The critical questions and answers relate directly to his yard training. If a "yes" response can be provided to each of the following questions, pup can be considered ready for field training:

1. Does he come when called?
2. Does he follow with a leash?
3. Does he follow without a leash?
4. Does he respond to the no, up and down commands? (Consider his size on up/down.)
5. Does he conduct himself properly in the carrier box (no barking or whining and entrance without hesitation)?

Only you, as owner-trainer, can determine if pup has the necessary disciplines. He will need these disciplines in order for you to exercise a measure of control over his actions and manage his behavior. The other commands are no less important but the above are the absolute minimum. If there is a no answer to any of these questions, pup would be better served with additional yard training.

Be prepared to insist that pup follow all commands. The field-training principles are essentially the same as yard training—simplicity, repetition, consistency, patience, gentleness, firmness and persistence. (See Chapter 4.)

During yard training, you have learned a great deal about pup and vice versa. You have successfully trained him to follow your commands. This will give you the needed self-confidence to put him through his paces in the field. Now it's time to load him in the carrier and introduce him to the new and exciting world of field work and rabbit hunting.

Chapter 7
Field Training: Stage I

Field Training Goals

As you begin to train pup in the field, think about what you want to accomplish with him. What goals do you want him to achieve?

First, you want him to learn to find or "start" rabbits on his own. This will require training him to look for rabbits where they live—in brush, log jams, brush piles and thickets. If pup is typical of most Beagle puppies, during the early stages of training he will exhibit the exact opposite tendencies. He will spend time looking out in the open fields and in the middle of farm roads.

Second, you want him to learn to identify rabbit scent lines and exhibit good trailing instincts. In this area, his heredity plays a major role. His instincts will determine the final outcome, and your job is to provide him adequate opportunities to react to identifiable rabbit scent lines.

Third, you will want to exercise a measure of control over his behavior by maintaining discipline with his learned voice commands. You may very well find yourself in a role more similar to a drill sergeant than a trainer, but discipline must be maintained.

Finally, you want him to learn to follow a scent line, barking (when he opens) until the rabbit is circled, intercepted or lost. There is considerable argument concerning the definition of a "started" pup. Is he started when he first "opens" (barks on a scent line)? Or is he started when he has proven he can trail a scent line sufficiently to circle a rabbit back to its original starting place? For our purposes, I will say pup is started when he can follow the scent line sufficiently, "tonguing" (barking) on the line, completely circling the rabbit back to the general area from which it first started.

These goals may appear as very tall orders for pup, but they are not unrealistic. After all, pup's bloodlines are in his favor. As long as you

Looks like this Beagle has picked up an exciting new scent to investigate. Photo courtesy of Anderson's Big Creek Kennels.

provide him the opportunities he will progress. Field training is an exciting adventure. When pup has successfully "opened" on his first rabbit, you will experience the excitement and satisfaction of knowing you played a major role in his development. When he completely circles his first rabbit you will feel the pride and amazement that can only result from all the hard work and training that you and pup have endured.

Field training is vastly different from yard training in several ways. The environmental change is the most obvious. During yard training, you were able to exercise considerable control over pup's actions. However, as he develops as a hunter in the field, you will need to relinquish some of this control and allow him to be guided by his bloodlines and natural instincts.

Another important difference is that field training requires you to learn to read rabbit signs. Locating and getting pup into choice places that hold rabbits is extremely important if he is going to learn to work rabbit scent lines. For the uninitiated, look for rabbit droppings (small round pellets) near the edge of fields, fencerows, thick brush, weedy areas and brush piles. In addition, rabbit tracks tell you immediately the rabbits are using a particular area. In brush or weeded areas, look for runs or small paths leading into and through briar patches, tangles of brush and honeysuckle. If you are training during winter months, with snow covering the ground, these signs are fairly obvious. If not, you will need to take the time to identify these signs and get pup as close to these areas as possible.

It's time to introduce pup to the exciting world of field work. Photo courtesy of Mike Baskerville, Jonesboro AR.

He may react to the scent in an excited manner or he may take a more casual approach.

Unlike yard training, there is no need to place time restrictions on field exercises. In field training, the more practice pup gets, the better. However, you will need to recognize when pup begins to tire. So don't push him beyond his physical limitations (or yours) and plan your field work accordingly. Usually, puppies began to tire and become bored after three or four hours, but it varies from puppy to puppy. Good judgment will be needed on this point.

Pup will need at least one trip per week to provide him with sufficient field work for him to become a competent hunter. Other obligations may make it difficult for this goal to be realized, but set the target at one field trip a week and go for it.

The First Trips

These first trips, if typical, will be exploratory for pup. The field is a new world for him. There are literally hundreds of new sights, sounds and scents for him to explore and learn. So keep your expectations reasonable. Anyone who has been around hound men, especially Beagle houndsmen, has heard the exaggerated story of the "Super Pup" who hit the field for the first time and "opened" (barked) on the first scent line almost immediately. Just so you won't be disappointed and discouraged, take these stories very lightly. Don't expect pup to perform on that level immediately. The real world dictates otherwise, with success resulting from time, hard work and practice. If your Beagle happens to perform at "Super Pup" level, he is worth a fortune.

As a general rule, pup will need many exploratory trips, and it may be as long as a year before he opens on a scent line. Not all puppies require that much time, but many do. Much depends on his abilities, bloodlines and training opportunities. The key is to expose him to rabbit scent lines as frequently as possible and let nature take its course. You will need patience, and he needs all the practice he can get.

On pup's first trip, he is going to be a little awkward and perhaps even timid. When you put him on the ground, lead him to a safe area away from the roads. Remove the leash. Get him to follow you where ever you go without the leash. Go slowly. Give him time to investigate the many scents that are available. The novice trainer must realize that nearly everything in nature has a unique scent and pup needs to familiarize himself with all of them. Many of these scents vary in accordance with the seasons of the year. Others remain constant. At any rate, patience will be necessary for pup to get the opportunity to sort out the myriad of different scents to his satisfaction.

Walk with him through the high weeds and grass. Locate a small ditch, one that will require him to jump across it. When you reach the ditch, simply step across, walk a few paces and call him to you. He will probably hesitate and whine, but continue walking slowly away from him. At the same time, call him to you with the come command. After several minutes of hesitation, his eagerness to be near you will overcome his fear

If pup gets his feet wet, so much the better.

of the water-filled ditch. He will then either jump across or splash through the mud and water to reach you. If he gets wet and muddy, so much the better. He needs to get accustomed to getting his feet wet anyway. When he catches up with you, give him plenty of praise.

Attempt to locate some inclines, such as large ditch banks or small hills, or anything that will require him to use his back legs and feet. Make several trips up and down these inclines and get him to follow you. He will benefit greatly, both by developing those rear leg muscles and by to learning to overcome his natural fear of heights.

Find some rough terrain and get pup to follow you through it. These areas can be canebreaks, brush, honeysuckle or briar patches and swamp areas. If you are training during a primary season (late fall, winter or early spring), walk trough the rough areas and encourage pup to follow. The object of this exercise is to help pup learn that rabbits are usually found in the rough places. Keep pup's size in mind and don't ask him to do something he is physically incapable of doing.

The Field Command "Up"

As was mentioned in Chapter 5, the up command is important to pup's field training. He has learned during yard training to respond to the command to get into the carrier box. The field version of the exercise, however, is designed to help him learn to scale fences.

For this exercise, you need to locate an overgrown fence line that is composed of mesh wire (squares along the lower section and two or three strands of barbed wire along the top). Many of these old fence rows are dilapidated and covered with vegetation. These are ideal rabbit areas because they offer plenty of food, cover and escape routes. Rabbits love them. When pursued, the rabbit can weave in and out of the mesh wire in an attempt to lose his pursuer. A clean fence row can be used for this exercise but a covered one is preferred.

When you approach the fence row, locate a place where you can cross without great difficulty. You will need to have pup's leash readily available. Cross the fence and walk slowly away, leaving pup behind on the opposite side. Pup's initial reaction will be frustration. He will whine, howl or even bark. You need to ignore all of these antics temporarily. Call him to come and give the command, "up, puppy." Pup may or may not try to follow the up command at first. Wait about four seconds, (count them) and give the command, "up, puppy, come." Repeat this routine at least eight times.

If pup fails to respond appropriately at the end of the eighth sequence, walk back to the fence and cross over to his side of the fence. Place pup on the leash and cross to the opposite side, feeding the leash between the barbed wire strands and the mesh wire. Be sure that pup has room between the mesh and the barbed wire to get through without injury.

Now give the command, "up, puppy," and gently pull on the leash in an upward motion. By now, pup should have his front feet on the top of the mesh, with enough room for him to get his head under the barbed wire. If he refuses to climb the mesh, reach over with your free hand, placing it under his tail and gently lift him between the barbed and mesh wires, giving the up command each time. Repeat this routine 10 times.

By now, pup should be getting between the mesh and barbed wires without assistance. Each time he gets across, with or without help, give him plenty of praise. Practice this exercise on each field trip until he can cross a fence without help or hesitation.

If pup finds a hole in the mesh on his own and crosses without help, that's just fine. But practice the fence-crossing routine anyway using the up-puppy-come command each time you take him to the field. He needs to learn to find a convenient hole to get through, but at some point he will need to learn to go over the top of the mesh. These exercises will help him learn and decrease his frustration.

Eating Carrion and How to Stop It

Inevitably, pup is going to find something undesirable and attempt to eat it. Most puppies are victims of this odd behavior and it's best to correct the problem in the early stages of his training. Exploratory field trips provide excellent opportunities to train him to leave certain tempting items well enough alone.

Pup is beginning to learn that his nose is a marvelous locator. He will quickly learn to locate these items by scenting. Some of these tempting tidbits are quite repulsive, such as dead birds, frogs, turtles, rats, mice and household waste. Pup must learn to resist these appetizers and keep his mind on the business at hand. While the health risk from eating these items would probably be negligible, one can't be certain.

When pup happens upon one of these undesirable items and attempts to eat or chew it, take action immediately. Give the no command in a very sharp, commanding voice. Then call him to you. If he refuses to come or ignores you, go to him and remove the item from his mouth. Give the no command again. Usually, this will suffice until he happens upon another tasty morsel. Repeat the sequence each time he indulges in this behavior.

It will take many repetitions for pup to leave these undesirable items alone, but as his trainer you need to stay on top of it. Be patient, consistent and repetitious. He will eventually pass them by with only a casual sniff or ignore them completely, but only if you are persistent in your efforts.

Getting Pup Into the Brush

During these early exploratory trips, it will be important to get pup into the specific areas that hold rabbits. Rabbits by nature inhabit dense, covered brushy areas. Pup might be a little reluctant to tackle these ar-

The Check command can start with pup on a leash to teach him to explore.

eas on his own so he will need your help to learn to explore these areas.

When you have located training areas that hold rabbits, you will need to get pup into the middle of these thickets in order for him to learn to locate the game. In this exercise you will be teaching him by example. Be sure that you are dressed to protect yourself from the briars, stickers and thorns (see Chapter 6). The term "kicking them out" is very descriptive of what you will be doing.

The important point is getting pup to learn that you want him to work these areas by following a voice command. The command "check" is simple and effective. Other short commands that can be used are "look" and "find him." All three are effective and produce results. Whichever command you use, be consistent so pup will understand exactly what you expect him to do.

As you enter these covered areas, get pup to follow you. Encourage him to stay close to you by talking softly and smoothly, using words such as come, check and look. Provide frequent praise. Practice getting pup into these thick tangles each time you go afield with him. Just be sure you don't ask him to work an area that he is physically unable to handle.

His small size will allow him to operate amazingly well, but there are limits to what you can expect of him. As he grows and matures, you can raise your expectations accordingly.

A training area I use has a very large drainage ditch covered with canebreaks, honeysuckle, briar patches, thorns and tangles. The top of the ditch is about 30 feet from the water below. The sides of the ditch are extremely steep, virtually straight up and down in some places. Rabbits are located on these steep sides and an experienced dog has little trouble working these areas. However, knowing that dogs and puppies have a natural fear of heights, I bypass these steep areas while training a puppy and concentrate on more accessible areas where pup and I can maneuver without fear of falling. As the puppy gains experience and grows, he will be able to work steeper areas on his own.

As you practice this exercise, pup will get used to following you very closely. After four or five trips afield, he will begin to understand that you want him to get into the thick stuff because you are going into those places. When he eventually learns to hunt scent lines, all you will need to do is give the check command and point to an area with your free hand. He will then respond as commanded. Remember that this field work is a new world for him, so go slowly with consistency and patience.

Some owners might argue that pup will learn to work brush on his own and kicking out rabbits is just too much work and a waste of time. Perhaps so. On the other hand, if he hasn't been trained to look for rabbits where they live, how can you expect him to find them? How can you expect him to be dependable in finding rabbits instead of other game that is not wanted? Remember that pup needs to learn what you want him to hunt and where you want him to hunt for it.

Pup needs to learn to identify rabbit scent lines. These tangles and thickets are home to a variety of other critters. So how are you to know pup is working the correct scent line if it is not located for him? How can one be sure he isn't working the scent of a squirrel, raccoon or even a farm cat? To reduce the risk of this happening, this phase of his training will help minimize the risk and get him started right.

Here He Is!

After many field trips, pup will have learned to follow you into the thickets and tangles on a regular basis, responding to your check command. Each time you enter these areas now you will be looking for definite signs of rabbits. At some point, either accidentally or by design, a rabbit is going to flush from the tangles, offering an opportunity to get

Never let pup out of range of your hearing at any time for any reason. Photo courtesy of Mike Baskerville.

pup on a hot line. It is not important that pup actually see the rabbit because what you want him to learn at this stage is not what a rabbit looks like but rather what it smells like.

To get pup on the scent line, you will need a command that is unique and used only for getting him to come to the spot where the rabbit was last seen. The command should be given with a touch of enthusiasm in your voice, but don't overdo it. The command "Here he is" is excellent and produces results when properly used. Some trainers use "Tally Ho" or "That's him." These are excellent choices, and the command you select is simply a matter of personal preference. It's critically important to use the selected command only when you want pup to come to a positively identified scent line. It may be tempting to use the command to get pup to come when you are simply trying to get him to respond for some other reason. But don't yield to this temptation. This could result in pup not responding to scent lines and getting confused with the come command.

After the rabbit has flushed and you have positively identified it, call pup, using the command "Here he is" to the exact spot where the rabbit was last seen. Give the command with controlled excitement in your voice. Pup will recognize the excitement or at least get a clue that something different is happening. If pup refuses or balks at your command, go to him. Slip the leash over his neck and lead him to the spot. Once he is on the scent line, unleash him and step away one or two paces. Remain very quiet for a couple of minutes and watch his body react to the scent. If typical, his nose will be on the ground, his tail will be held straight up in the air and moving with a slight quiver. The longer he stays on the scent, the more his tail is apt to wag furiously. He may or may not attempt to follow the scent line. If he does, encourage him with your voice, but don't insist. Be patient and let him take his time. This is a new experience for him. He has probably never smelled anything like it before.

If by chance, pup saw the rabbit flush and wants to give chase, by all means let him do so. Once he loses or quits the chase, make a mental note of where the rabbit was last seen or where pup lost sight of it. Call him to the spot, using the command, "Here he is!"

Pup might react to rabbit scent excitedly or he may take a more casual approach. Whichever personality he exhibits, continue to flush rabbits for him. Pup learns by repetition, and in the case of trailing, by instinct. Therefore, the more rabbit scent lines he is exposed to, the sooner he will learn to follow the line, which is exactly what you want him to do. How many times will you need to flush rabbits for him before he begins to follow (trail)? No one knows for sure. It varies from puppy to puppy. Your task, as trainer, is to provide him with as many opportunities as possible and allow his natural trailing instincts to take over.

Occasionally, you will work hard to flush a rabbit and place pup on the line but he will totally ignore it. Why? This usually can be attributed to scenting conditions, and the explanations are based more on theory and speculation than actual scientific facts. Extremely dry, dusty conditions, coupled with low humidity, can often play a role. Melting snow appears to be another. One interesting theory is that the pregnant female rabbit excretes a special scent, making it difficult for predators to follow her line, thus protecting future offspring. Whatever the reason, you can be assured that pup knows more about what he smells than humans do. So, as a trainer, your only option is to expose him to as many scent lines as possible and trust him to make the right decisions.

When pup is placed on a scent line, allow him to spend as much time on it as he chooses. He may stay in one spot for several minutes or he may begin to trail. Either way, give him plenty of time to work with it. If he tires of the scent after several minutes and begins to ignore it, praise him for his work and attempt to get him back on the line again. If he refuses to respond, flush the rabbit (or another rabbit) and repeat the

"Here he is" command. After many repetitions, pup will learn that rabbit scent is what you want him to work and "Here he is" means a hot or fresh line.

Eventually, pup will regularly follow the lines of the rabbits that you flush. This is progress. Let him trail for as long and far as he desires. There is little need for you to help him. Just follow along behind him and keep him in sight. As he begins these trailing exercises, he will obviously be excited. His nose will be on the ground, his lower jaw and tongue working to keep saliva flowing and his tail wagging furiously. When he has trailed the line until he looses it, give him plenty of praise.

Occasionally, while trailing, pup will get turned around and backtrail or follow the scent line in a direction opposite to the rabbit's path. Simply leave pup to his own devices. The line will soon run out and pup will learn to reverse himself and return to the spot where he lost the scent.

Barking on the Scent Line

After many field training trips and what will seem like an eternity of kicking out or flushing rabbits for pup to trail, pup will suddenly react to a line with a bark. The tone of the bark will be distinctly different from the one pup uses when his territory is being threatened. Usually it will begin as a whine or whimper. Later, when pup matures, it may sound more like a howl or bawl. Some dogs have a deep, distinct bawl, while others possess more of a high-pitched or chopped-mouth sound. Which one pup exhibits will be determined by his genetics. It will not likely change much once he is a year old.

When pup first "strikes a line" (another term for finding a scent line), he may bark only once or twice. Then there will be silence. The reason for this is that pup doesn't really know what is happening to him. He may be surprised or even a little scared. The instinct is beginning to take over and this is a new and perhaps confusing experience for him. On the other hand, he may strike and trail for a considerable distance, tonguing (barking) constantly. Either way, when barking on a line begins, you and pup will have reached a major milestone in field training. This is the payoff for all the hard work and training. The emotion you will feel when pup first opens will be unforgettable. It is a mixture of amazement, excitement and pride. It can send shivers down your spine and make the hair on the back of your neck bristle. This signal tells you that pup is finally becoming a hunter of rabbits. Pup may be inefficient and his training incomplete, but he has become a rabbit hunter nevertheless. And you have played a major role in pup's accomplishment.

What pup needs now, more than ever, is practice, practice and more practice. He can only practice when provided opportunities. He learns nothing in the pen. Your role in providing these opportunities to practice will be the key to the development of pup's potential and his success as a hunting companion.

Working the Lines

Contrary to popular belief, the cottontail rabbit is not a dumb bunny. True, when frightened he will frequently freeze until the perceived danger has passed. It is also true that when pushed by predators,

Use the leash tactic to curtail misbehavior of any kind.

especially dogs, he will usually circle back to his home territory. But the circle he makes is frequently a series of loops, straight lines, zig-zags, and side jumps. Pup's challenge is to follow the line for as long and as far as necessary to bring the rabbit back to its general starting place. That is no simple feat when you think about it. Pup is following only a scent. His view of the world doesn't afford him the advantage of seeing around or over objects.

Being inexperienced, pup will lose the majority of these first lines, particularly if they are late-season rabbits that have survived being harassed by all sorts of varmints such as dogs, hunters, coyotes and other predators. They are wily and experienced. As a general rule, pup will trail and tongue his first few lines until the rabbit makes his first turn. The puppy may be prone to back trailing, which will complicate the situation even more. Let pup work out the back trailing as best he can. After about five minutes, you can help him by placing him on the line again if you know where the rabbit turned. If pup is extremely slow, he may lose the line as it grows cold. On the other hand, if he is extremely fast he may overrun the line when the rabbit loops or turns. When he loses the line, he will quit tonguing. He will then turn left or right, known as "casting," until his circle takes him back to the spot where he lost the line. How much time it takes him to cast, find the line and open again, is called a "check." These checks can last for a few seconds or several minutes. To be sure, the sooner he relocates the line, the better. The longer it takes, the colder the line becomes.

There is very little you can do as a trainer to help unless you have decided to follow pup on the line. This is acceptable but remember to give him plenty of time to work out the check by himself. If it becomes obvious he isn't going to find the line, you can intervene by placing him on it if you know the exact location or by helping him find another line by kicking out another rabbit. Eventually, as pup gains experience, he will learn to sort out the check on his own.

As pup works his first few lines, it's a good practice to keep him within sight and never let him get out of hearing. Follow 20-30 steps behind him, but resist interfering unless absolutely necessary. It's important for him to learn through experience. Remain quiet so you don't break his concentration. You can bet that pup is not going to circle the rabbit completely. The circling will come later as he matures and gains confidence. If he suddenly gives up the line or loses it and returns to you, give him plenty of praise. This reassures him that he is pleasing you. If you choose, you can flush the rabbit for him and let him begin the chase again. As he becomes more experienced, this tactic will not be necessary. Be patient. He is limited by size, genetics, inexperience and possibly scenting conditions. Given ample opportunity to practice, he will learn in time to encircle rabbits on his own.

Maintaining Discipline in the Field

Beagle owners are notorious for expecting perfection from their dogs. The ideal rabbit Beagle starts all his own rabbits, responds readily to and obeys all voice commands, never looses a line (thus eliminating checks), never runs any other game, circles every rabbit perfectly and efficiently, has the perfect tongue, retrieves all wounded game and never exhibits gun shyness. However, because this is an imperfect world, the perfect rabbit dog is always an illusion. You can train pup for perfection but attaining the goal will be forever elusive. But if pup likes to hunt and is willing to work at the task, he can be forgiven for any shortcomings. He will make plenty of mistakes and disappointments are inevitable. (This also applies to the trainer.) But a pup who enjoys the hunt will more than make up for mistakes and lack of ability.

Whether perfect or not, as a trainer you will need to maintain discipline in the field. During yard training, pup learned a number of voice commands, such as come, sit, and sit-stay. These disciplines provide you some control over his behavior. It is very important for pup to practice these basic disciplines while in the field. As trainer, you will need to be vigilant and keep pup on his toes. You might need to develop a voice similar to a military drill sergeant to accomplish this task, but that's okay. Remember, never use corporal punishment. Never strike pup for any reason. Be patient.

One voice command that can cause a trainer, especially a novice trainer, considerable concern, is come. As trainer, you expect pup to respond as he did in the yard. But let's be practical. Asking him to come while he is hunting a scent line or trailing a line is asking him to do the impossible. Pup is a victim of his heredity and instincts. His inbred hound instincts demand he trail until the rabbit is intercepted or lost. On the other hand, he has been trained to respond to your command. Usually, heredity and instinct will win over trained habits. However, if he is simply goofing off or runs 100 yards ahead of you for no apparent reason, that's a totally different matter. In this situation, call him to you. If he refuses, make the extra effort to catch him and place him on the leash for five minutes. Command him to the sit or sit- stay position and insist that he do so. Suspending his hunting privilege temporarily will get his attention in short order. When you leash him, say, "no," so he knows you are displeased with his behavior.

Using the leash tactic to curtail misbehavior of any kind will keep him within his learned disciplines. Just be sure that you reward him with praise when he performs correctly. Pup is smart enough to know that good performance gets him positive rewards while misbehavior will result in the loss of his hunting privileges. Again, patience, persistence and consistency on your part are the critical elements.

The leash tactic can also be used when pup opens on game other than rabbits. In the early stages of field training, until he gains self-confidence and maturity, pup may be guilty of opening on quail, squirrels, woodcock, fox, deer, raccoons or other animals. You will need to react quickly to correct these indiscretions by sharply giving the no command and placing him on the leash for the five-minute minimum. Pup must learn that he is to hunt rabbits and only rabbits. As he gains hunting experience, the no command itself will usually be sufficient to stop him, but don't hesitate to use the leash if he refuses any of your commands.

Now pup is on his way to developing into an efficient hunting companion. This first phase of his training will remain with him for the duration of his life. He now needs practice. Practice comes with opportunity. Opportunity can be provided only by you, the trainer. As a rule, the more time you spend with pup in the field, the more time you will want to spend with him. It's good for both of you.

Chapter 8
Field Training - Stage II

Review of Stage I

During stage I training, pup learned the fundamentals of what the world of rabbit hunting is all about. He has learned to follow you, overcome fences, ignore carrion, respond to your check and here-he-is commands, open on a rabbit scent line and follow the scent line as far as his size and experience allow. And he behaves himself as you command. He is now ready for stage II of his training.

Expectations for Stage II

It is important to note that there often is no clear line of demarcation between stage I and stage II training but rather a blending of both stages. Generally, stage II marks the end of his first year in the field and the beginning of his second hunting season. It depends primarily on pup's learned abilities. Many of the essential skills pup learned his first year will remain with him for a lifetime, such as response to the commands check and here he is. Problems, such as eating carrion and crossing fences, should occur less frequently because pup now has the field experience necessary to handle these situations on his own. You will occasionally need to remind or help him but it will be the exception rather than the rule.

Stage II training includes getting pup into good physical condition, training him to start rabbits on his own, training him to hunt within a reasonable range, working over the gun, hunting him with your hunting companions, handling the problems of the second-year-dog ailment and a guide for the trainer to recognize hazards while afield.

Stage I and Stage II blend together. Photo courtesy of Anderson's Big Creek Kennels, Jonesboro AR.

Getting Pup Into Good Physical Condition

Pup has now completed a season in the field and unless you have opted for year-round field training, it's a sure bet that he is out of shape. This results from all that pen time during the hot-weather weeks. He has been spending most of his time lying around the pen, sleeping, drinking and eating. The only physical demands placed upon him are the various yard training exercises you have been putting him through. These soft exercises may keep him mentally sharp but they don't do much to get him into hunting form.

Much like an athlete, pup will need to work himself into good physical condition gradually. If you allow him to run for as long as he wants on the first day afield, you risk pup becoming foot-sore, muscle-strained and exhausted. Providing his nutritional level has been maintained, the following schedule should put him in top form after five or six field trips:

Allow no more than one hour of field work on the first trip. Increase the allotted time 15-30 minutes each succeeding trip, up to a maximum of four hours. At the completion of the four-hour trip, he should be ready for a full day in the field and be able to withstand the mental and physical rigors of hunting without undue stress. The first trip after several weeks in the pen may be more comparable to a teenager's bedroom than an organized field run. But many of the problems caused by pup's over-excitement can be controlled if you have maintained his verbal commands during the off season.

On these first field runs of the year, remember to allow pup some play time. It is as important for him to enjoy being in the field with you as it is for him to produce. Much like a child, pup can become stressed by intense training and these playtimes become mental breaks for him. Go slowly. Let pup work at his own pace. Sure, you want him to get into shape, but there is no harm in allowing him a little fun in the process.

Starting Rabbits On His Own

To this point, each time you have taken pup afield, you have gotten into the thick stuff with him. He has learned to follow you everywhere. Basically, you have taught him where to look for rabbits by example. He is now beginning to learn that rabbits really do live in the heavy cover. He has learned to respond to the check command and has been introduced to scent lines. Perhaps he has not completely circled a rabbit, but it is beginning to sink into his brain that the rabbit is what you and he are looking for.

Now when you put him down, let him follow you to the choice areas that hold rabbits. As you approach one of these areas, give the check command and wait for his response. If he refuses to explore, coax him with your voice. If that fails, slip the leash over his head and lead him to the area, talking quietly to him while doing so. When he is in the thick stuff, unleash him and watch him closely. Look for him to start tunneling through the tangles. If he does check out the area, even if he only goes a few steps and returns, give him plenty of praise. After many repetitions, pup is going to understand that getting into the brush brings two rewards. One is that he will get verbal praise even if he fails to find a scent line. The other is that he might jump a rabbit or strike a hot scent line. Either way, he has a no-lose situation.

One of the main reasons for owning a hunting dog is for the dog to find the game. There will be times when you will need to get into the thickets and tangles to help him move rabbits because of adverse scenting or weather conditions. But to start the rabbits moving is pup's primary job. By providing him with ample practice opportunities, he should be starting rabbits on his own after a maximum of 10 weeks of field training. Again, caution is advised on expectations. Puppies learn at different rates. Some are better start dogs than others. Some are better trail dogs than start dogs. You can bet that if you start all of pup's rabbits for him, he will be totally satisfied with the arrangement. Keep him on the job of

Junior may stay close to you. Don't be alarmed. Photo courtesy of
Mike Baskerville.

starting. Experience shows that if pup starts his own rabbit, it gives him
an incentive to stay on the line longer. The more practice he gets, the
better he will become at the task.

Hunting Within Reasonable Range

Getting pup to hunt close to you is of major importance. If he does not
learn to hunt with you, it's almost certain that at some point you will be
hunting for him. A part of this learning process begins in stage I when
pup is learning to check areas at your command. He has become accustomed to your voice. He has developed a sense of wanting to be near you.
He is comfortable being within the sound of your voice even if he can't
see you.

When pup hits the brush and thickets, verbally encourage him to find
rabbits. He will sense you are with him and the encouragement will fire
his enthusiasm. Call it relationship enhancement or simple companionship if you wish. The point is that pup wants to please you. Through the

encouragement he gets from you, he becomes a team member. If he can't see you, he still knows you are there because he can hear you.

Let him work an area for several minutes. If he doesn't strike a line, call him to you. If he fails to come when commanded, locate him and put him on a leash for five minutes. Then begin again. Pup will eventually learn that he is expected to hang close over a period of time. The length of time it takes depends upon his personality and experience as well as the patience of the trainer. But pup needs to learn to show himself periodically. It will take time, but through repetition and persistence he will learn that if he isn't trailing and tonguing on a line, he has to let you know his whereabouts. Don't push him too hard on this exercise. Firmness, gentleness, patience and consistency are the paramount keys. Don't be mislead in thinking this is an easy exercise. Getting pup to hunt with you can try your patience. But the payoff is worth the effort. After many trials, pup will hunt with you as a matter of habit if you are repetitious in your efforts.

It is important not to forget that pup knows more than you do about scent and scenting conditions. He may be cold-trailing and working hard to get close enough to the rabbit so the scent is strong enough to trigger his instinct to open. This requires you to use your best judgment in allowing him to range out away from you, but you need to know him well enough to determine whether he is working a line or just messing around. In a nutshell, there will be times when you will just have to trust him to strike out on his own. How far is too far? That's a matter of trainer preference. If he is used to working near you, it will be much easier to manage him. However, if he is allowed total freedom in his ranging, the rabbit he jumps may be so far away that you will spend most of your time trying to find him and the rabbit.

Working Over the Gun

From a practical point, pup is expected to hunt and put rabbits before the gun and eventually, depending upon the shooter's skill, into the bag. But shooting over him before he is ready can cause problems. There are literally hundreds of books describing methods of curing gun-shyness. They are excellent reference materials. However, many of them deal with the problem from viewpoint of the trainer rather than the dog.

Pup may or may not be gun-shy but you will know the first time you attempt to shoot in his presence. Assume he is gun-shy and look at the problem from his point of view. Imagine that you are walking along a quiet neighborhood street minding your own business. Suddenly, someone sets off a charge of dynamite right beside you. You panic for a moment. Your head aches and your ears are ringing. Your first reactions would probably be to head for cover, check to see if you are still in one piece and wonder what in thunder happened. Should it be any different for pup when he hears a shotgun blast for the first time? If he is less than six months old, he is probably going to head for cover immediately. You may spend considerable time locating him as a result of this unexpected blast.

A good procedure, if not overused, is to introduce pup to gun noise gradually. Before you begin, check your state hunting regulations dealing with the carrying of firearms outside of regular hunting seasons, if you are training during closed seasons. Assuming there is no legal problem, use a small-caliber firearm such as a .22 rifle or pistol and tie pup to a tree or other stationary object. Walk about 30 steps away and fire. Pup will probably flinch at the first shot. Go to him immediately and calm him with a soothing voice and gentle hands. This exercise works even

Pup needs to learn to work over the gun.

better if you have someone else do the firing while you hold pup on the leash. Nevertheless, repeat the exercise six to eight times. After each shot, reassure him that everything is okay. After 15 sessions, pup should not be exhibiting more than a slight flinch.

The next step is to increase the noise by replacing the .22 with a shotgun. Just be certain to reassure pup after each shot that the noise is harmless. Over time, pup will get used to the sound of the blast and show no negative reactions. A word of caution: After completing 15 sessions using the shotgun, refrain from shooting rabbits in front of him until you are thoroughly convinced he won't react negatively to the noise. He must be thoroughly convinced that the noise won't harm him.

After pup has overcome his fear of gunshot noise, it's perfectly acceptable to shoot a rabbit he has started, even if he hasn't completely circled it. When the rabbit is down, don't pick it up immediately. Give pup ample time to follow the scent line to the dead rabbit. If he should lose the line, leave the rabbit where it lays and place pup on the scent line where you first saw the rabbit. Allow pup to find the rabbit from that point. When he reaches it, allow him to "mouth" and play with it for a few minutes. Using as much excitement as possible, pour on the praise. This will help him recognize that the object of the game is a downed rabbit. This praise will also help reduce any fear of gunshots he may be harboring.

Allowing pup to mouth and play with a downed rabbit will help you coach him to retrieve game. When pup finds the rabbit, command, "get it, pup," and call him to you. Most puppies love the attention of this new game and will pick the rabbit up off the ground and hold it high in the air. After picking up the rabbit, pup will probably want to strut around with it. Try to get him to bring it to you, even if it is only a few steps. When he completes this task, pour on the praise again. Pup will eventually learn to catch and retrieve wounded game, even when he can't see you. Another word of caution: If pup should have a tendency to run away with the rabbit or shred it with his teeth, it's advisable to dispense with this exercise.

The Second-Year-Dog Ailment

Well into pup's second season, you may note some startling changes in his disposition, development and behavior. For the novice owner/trainer, these changes can be extremely perplexing and confusing. To this point, pup has been totally loyal and reliable. He followed voice commands, behaved in the company of other dogs and people and has been a lot of fun to work with.

Now, during his second season, it appears that at times he takes complete leave of his senses. He ignores your commands to come, constantly attempts to hunt on his own out of sight and hearing, jumps up on others, sneaks off to run with packs of dogs, refuses to respond to the here-he-is command, and in general becomes obstinate and bullheaded.

Discouragement and disappointment begin to invade your thought processes. You frequently find yourself questioning whether you have lost the ability to train him. Unthinkable terms begin to occupy your mind, such nuisance, untrainable and worthless. You are disheartened by this direct attack on your self-esteem and self-confidence and ability as a trainer. The thought of just throwing in the towel and starting over with a new puppy is crossing your mind.

But all is not lost. Who ever said that Beagles were not stubborn? Any trainer who has worked Beagles has found himself at this point of near-desperation. Be assured there is hope for both you and pup. No one can say for certain exactly what makes pup act this way, but be assured it is neither permanent nor terminal. There is a theory to help explain pup's unusual behavior.

Under this theory, pup has reached adolescence because one year of a dog's life is considered equal to seven years in human life. This being the case, pup is equivalent to a 13- or 14-year-old human. Teenagers commonly display such characteristics as confusion, rebellion and self-searching for independence. These characteristics usually frustrate even the most dedicated parent. The youngster who has previously conformed to the wishes, rules and values of his parents with loyalty and cooperation suddenly finds himself questioning parental judgment, authority and perhaps even their sanity. This does not indicate failure in the parent. It is part of the normal cycle of life.

Pup is in much the same situation. He still wants to please you but he also wants to prove to himself that he can do things on his own and in his own way. Coupled with his inherited stubbornness, which he cannot control, his actions mirror those of the developing teenager.

Frustrating for a trainer? Absolutely! As trainer, you are suddenly the parent of a rebellious teenager. And it will test your training skills and patience to the limit.

You must remain patient, firm and consistent to resolve this temporary problem, and a sense of humor doesn't hurt. Just as the teenager eventually grows through his stage and evolves into a mature adult, so will it be with pup. Getting through the stage may be difficult to manage sometimes, but both you and pup will learn and grow from the experience.

Pup can be trained to retrieve wounded game.

It matters little how many Beagles you train, each one will eventually experience these second-year-dog maladies. Be assured that it does not detract from your abilities as a trainer.

Hunting Pup With Your Partners

By now, pup is starting rabbits on his own with only occasional help from you. He is tonguing on the line, circling rabbits more or less consistently and has become accustomed to working over the gun. He is quickly becoming a complete hunting companion. You are understandably proud of him and yourself for these accomplishments.

The most natural impulse is to invite a good friend or hunting buddy

Insist that all members of your party wear at least a blaze orange vest. Photo courtesy of Mike Baskerville.

to accompany you on a hunt. One of the finer aspects of having a well-trained hunting Beagle is the opportunity to share the hunting experience with others.

A suggestion: Don't brag too much about pup. Hunting dogs frequently manage to have an off day on the very day you decide to set up a hunt.

Nevertheless, set some ground rules about safety and dog handling before you get into the field. If your friend is experienced in hunting over dogs, there will be few if any problems as he will surely understand the following rules. However, if he lacks experience hunting with dogs it is best to advise him before the hunt. Keep things simple but insist that the rules be followed without question to insure a quality hunting experience. While not all inclusive, the following rules can serve as a guide:

1. Everyone in the hunting party, and that includes the trainer, will wear a blaze orange vest. (Keep spares in your vehicle for those who forget theirs.) Those who refuse can kindly remain at the vehicle until the hunt is completed.

2. The trainer, and only the trainer, will give commands to pup unless directed otherwise in specific situations. Example: If another hunter happens to jump a rabbit you might want him to give the command, "Here he is!" However, any discipline and all other handlings of pup will be the sole responsibility of the trainer. Period.

3. Pup will not be allowed to jump up on people or dogs under any circumstances. The no command and a five-minute leash penalty can curtail this misbehavior quickly.

4. Others can pet or encourage pup, but not while he is working to find a scent line. Petting and other acts of affection should be confined to breaks or while loading or unloading.

5. Decide if "jump shooting" will be allowed. For the uninitiated, jump shooting is firing at a rabbit that has been jumped either by pup or a member of the hunting party but has not been circled. This decision should be made after considering pup's reaction to gunshot noise, the scenting conditions, fairness of the chase, and hazards such as the number of hunters in the party. As a general rule, jump shooting should not be allowed because an important part of the sport is to allow pup to work the rabbit for as long as possible. But exceptions can be made. Just be sure everyone in the hunting party knows your wishes ahead of time.

6. If pup begins to get out of hearing range, the trainer will assume the responsibility of retrieving him. As owner/trainer, this is your responsibility. Advise others before the hunt that if pup moves off at a distance beyond hearing, you will handle the situation. If others want to accompany you, that's fine. But pup is your dog. It's your responsibility to control him.

These basic rules will help make for a pleasant outdoor experience. The list is not exhaustive by any means, and you might prefer to add others. The important point is that pup will probably not obey anyone else, so why confuse him and your hunting friends as well? Generally, if others have previously hunted with Beagles, they can be relied upon not to interfere. But there may be occasions when this guide will help you and others to spend quality hunting time together.

Recognizing Training and Hunting Hazards

During pup's first year of training, hazards were few because he was usually close by your side. This allowed you to work him in small areas where rabbits were plentiful and there was little risk that he would range out of sight or hearing.

But now pup has matured and has become accustomed to ranging further away from you in search of his quarry. When he strikes a line he will concentrating completely on his business, which is following the scent until the rabbit is intercepted. Neither the rabbit nor the dog will be particularly concerned with possible hazards during the race. They are both responding to their instincts, the rabbit to escape and pup to follow the

Basic rules help make for a pleasant outdoor experience.

scent line. But hazards do exist and whenever possible you will want to avoid them, keeping pup safe and your field experience enjoyable.

One of the most common hazards is automobile traffic. How many times have you driven down a highway or country road and thought about a rabbit suddenly crossing the road in front of you with a dog or pack of dogs in pursuit? Probably not often. This is precisely why roads and highways need to be avoided. If you, as an owner/trainer, rarely think about a dog following a rabbit as it crosses in front of your automobile, other drivers probably never think about it. If you are familiar with your hunting and training areas, road hazards can be avoided with a little effort. The problem arises when using unfamiliar territory. By keeping pup within hearing distance at all times, you can usually determine when a rabbit is moving in the direction of a roadway. You can then intercept pup before he reaches the road and leash him. Remember, no rabbit is worth the risk of getting pup injured by an unsuspecting motorist. There are always rabbits elsewhere.

Be on the alert for traplines, unexpected hazards that can give pup a great deal of grief. Trapping activities are usually regulated by state fish and game departments, and the rules are often listed in your general hunting regulations. Read them. Be familiar with the trapping seasons in your area and be aware of the dangers they can present. Some states require traplines to be marked with brightly colored streamers. Others do not. Some states require that they be located out of paths, trails and runways commonly used by persons, dogs or other domestic animals.

One of my former rabbit-hunting areas included a large drainage ditch constructed by the Army Corps of Engineers. The ditch was bordered by a harvested soybean field and the banks were covered with honeysuckle, cane thickets, briar patches and other tangles, all of which combined to provide excellent rabbit cover. The ditch contained slow-moving water, and the average depth was five feet. Unknown to me at the time, it also contained a healthy population of muskrat and other fur-bearing game. I was also unaware that a local trapper had set underwater smooth jaw, leg-hold traps several feet from the bank. They were well hidden and the trapline was unmarked—all perfectly legal.

My youngest son, Roy, and I put my male/female Beagle pair, Sam and Bell, down at the edge of the bank at mid-afternoon. In a short time, Sam struck a hot scent line. The cottontail flushed ahead about 100 yards away, darting out of the tangles into the cut soybean field and then back into the cover of the bank. Bell, who had been working behind him, immediately honored his found line and joined the race. The rabbit continued along the bank for another 200 yards with the dogs tonguing the entire time. Then came the inevitable check when the line was lost. Everything was quiet. Within a couple of minutes I heard Sam scream with pain. Roy remarked that Sam had evidently found the line again, but I knew instinctively that something was very wrong.

Seconds later, I heard Bell let out a scream and I knew that both dogs were in big trouble. Filled with anxiety, I quickly unloaded my gun and ran to the top of the bank, with Roy following a few steps behind me. When I reached the scene, both dogs were several feet from the bank, howling, screaming and thrashing in the water. I quickly assessed the situation and realized they were both caught in underwater traps.

I quickly handed my gun to Roy, stripped off my outer hunting clothes and waded out to Sam. He was nearly exhausted and barely able to keep his head above water. As I held him above the water with my left arm under his midsection, I was able to free him from the five-inch, smooth-jawed, leg-held trap and carried him to the bank. I leashed him and left him with Roy and waded back into the water to release Bell.

By the time I reached her, she was in a state of total frenzy from fear and the pain. I attempted to release her in the same manner as I had released Sam. But the trap jaws would not budge. Out of pain and fear, Bell bit down on my arm doing no damage. I felt under the dark water with my left hand and found the holding chain and stake. I pulled them out of the muddy bottom and carried dog, trap, chain and stake to the bank. Seconds later, I had Bell free.

Luckily, neither dog was seriously injured in the episode, but the hunt came to an abrupt halt. Since that terrifying experience, I make a point to familiarize myself with the trapping regulations and seasons. I avoid traplines wherever I find them. If I spot a trap, marked or unmarked, I move to another area.

This experience also emphasizes the importance of knowing where your dogs are at all times. You can't always know the trapline hazard, but if you spot this danger call pup in and move to another area.

Electric fences can also create a hazard. These fences are usually found where livestock are prevalent. Most often, the electric fence will consist of a single strand of light colored wire, with small round circular holders spaced at regular intervals. Some of these electric strands are placed near the top strands of fences, while others are placed at or near the lower strands of regular wires. The voltage is usually not sufficient enough to injure a dog or human, nevertheless it's best to develop a healthy respect for them. More often than not, your feet will be wet and your hands moist. So, don't touch the wire.

Keeping pup away from these wires can be difficult. He is a hunter, not a master electrician. He has absolutely no sense about the dangers. If he is wet and touches the wire (usually with his tail), he will probably sustain a mild shock with no permanent damage. But to play it safe, move to another area. If pup gets a shock, mild though it may be, his enthusiasm for the hunt will be greatly reduced. Field experience shows when a dog has been hurt or injured while hunting a particular area, if returned to the same area later to hunt, hazard or not, he will sense the surroundings and his performance will be lackluster at best.

A situation that occasionally arises during training and hunting is a pup's tendency to want to join other packs of running dogs or even a single strange dog. This is hazardous in several ways. These unknown dogs may be docile and healthy but one can't be sure. The owner may be ethical and never think of taking pup, but that's not certain either. It's best to play it safe and try to avoid allowing pup to be put in a compromising situation. If he hears or sees these other dogs and shows an interest in joining them, give the no command immediately. If he fails to respond, place him on the leash and, if necessary, relocate to another area. Remember that because pup is trained makes him a target for unscrupulous thieves in the field, so take the necessary precautions, even if it requires the inconvenience of relocation.

Thin ice can also pose safety problems. During winter months in some sections of the country, cold weather can freeze water rapidly but within a few hours a warming trend can begin a slight thaw of the skim ice. When pup strikes a line or jumps a rabbit, the rabbit will frequently cross these thin ice areas to escape quickly. Pup will automatically follow the line and break through the ice because he is heavier than the rabbit. Although pup has the natural ability to swim, the thin layer of ice can prevent him from pulling himself out of the water. Most of the time, he will reverse himself and return to shore. The greatest danger is when he becomes exhausted. If the water is deep with a swift undercurrent, as is common with rivers, he may get caught under the ice and not be able to return. Whenever possible, avoid these areas when weather patterns fluctuate and return there when the weather is more acceptable.

Hunting and training near residences create a special set of problems. On his own, pup cannot obey such signs as *Keep Out* and *Beware of Dog*. As owner/trainer, be aware of residences in and near your training and hunting areas and keep pup away from them. Respect residents by intercepting pup before he gets close to them. Some folks don't appreciate the howling and baying of strange dogs disturbing their peace and quiet.

Many of these residents have dogs of their own. When pup is tonguing on a line, house dogs frequently react to the sound by making even more noise. So keep your eyes and ears on pup and simultaneously be aware of these dwellings. If pup gets close to one, intercept him as quickly as possible. Avoiding the problem is highly preferable to facing an irate citizen who has just been rudely awakened because you failed to control your dog.

Hazards in the field are almost too numerous to mention. Changing weather conditions, railroads, automobiles, dwellings, fences and traps are just a sampling. You cannot avoid hazards totally, but the key in most cases is awareness and avoidance. Learn to recognize hazards in your area and do your best to avoid them. Remember that pup is totally your responsibility. He can't think or reason for himself, so you have to make judgments and decisions for him. Knowing the territory helps, but in new territory, anything can happen. So learn to develop a sixth sense that will help you recognize hazards and take the necessary precautions to avoid them.

You and pup have now come full circle in training. Pup will continue to improve with practice and experience—if he has enough opportunities. Only you can provide him with these opportunities. He is not yet a veteran; most dogs usually reach their peak hunting ability in their fourth or fifth season. But he is on his way. Your biggest problem now will be finding enough time to get him out in the field.

Chapter 9
The Second Dog

Pup is now regularly starting and circling rabbits. Sure, he may be guilty of making mistakes but he is loyal and enjoys hunting. Your field experiences are now very rewarding. Beagles and rabbit hunting are in your blood. Happiness is watching and listening to pup work a scent line from start to finish.

So why consider acquiring a second Beagle? Arriving at this decision is not always easy. There can be many reasons to get a brace mate to run with pup. If you are considering the idea and are struggling with the decision, the following pros and cons may help you make a decision.

The Pros

First, a look at the reasons why you might consider adding a second dog:

Pup works hard in the field but you have begun to notice that he loses a considerable number of scent lines because he is too slow on the line (which allows the line to grow cold) or he pushes the rabbit too fast and frequently overruns the line (resulting in excessive checks or loss of the line entirely). Perhaps a hunting partner or brace mate might improve pup's performance and result in moving rabbits on a more consistent basis.

Perhaps pup is a little weak in his ability to start rabbits, resulting in a great deal of your time being spent in kicking them out. Perhaps two dogs could do a better job.

You may have considered what you would do if something unfortunate happened to pup. If he were stolen, lost, or suffered a crippling injury, you would be without a hunting companion. Or maybe pup is getting up in years, say seven or eight. If so, a replacement will be needed eventually. Beagles usually reach their peak as hunters in their

There can be many reasons to get a brace mate.

fifth year. They will hold this peak for about two years before changes are noticed. Some Beagles, given proper diet and care, can live and hunt to age 12 and 13, but their skills begin to deteriorate in the eight or ninth year.

Acceptance is usually a simple process. Photo courtesy of Anderson's Big Creek Kennel, Jonesboro AR.

You have had the experience of successfully training pup. There will be some differences in training a second beagle, but the yard training is essentially the same. The kennel and other facilities are already in place. If a partition was not installed in the pen when it was originally constructed, it's a fairly simple job to install one. You now have a basic knowledge of dog care and have an established veterinarian. Training areas are available because you have developed good relationships with a number of land owners. You undoubtedly know at least one Beagle owner who has a puppy available for sale and you are familiar with the selection process. Most important of all the reasons to obtain that brace mate for pup is the pure enjoyment of the sport—training, working and hunting Beagles. The thrill of listening to a brace of beagles working a hot scent line is reason enough.

The Cons

Some of the reasons for not obtaining that second dog:

You may not have enough time for a thorough training program. Job responsibilities may prevent you from allotting the needed hours. Perhaps family members are opposed to the idea. This can happen when someone else is burdened with the primary responsibility for care and feeding. Perhaps your personal situation simply does not allow a second dog. Whatever the reason, it is always a very personal decision. However, for those who want that brace mate for pup, what follows is designed to help you and junior get started right.

An important point to remember is that unless you are a better-than-average trainer, I recommend that pup have a minimum of two solo hunting seasons before you add the second dog. The reason is that pup and junior will be penned and learning to work together as a team. You will want to use pup as an assistant in portions of the field exercises. With two seasons of hunting experience, pup will gain maturity and develop a sufficient amount of discipline and concentration so he won't be totally distracted by junior.

I also recommend that you acquire junior at the beginning of an off season to allow plenty of time for him to learn his yard-training exercises. For example, if you purchase him in early or late spring, you can yard train him during the warm summer months without undue haste. If you obtain him during the fall or winter seasons, he will certainly want to accompany you and pup on your trips afield. If this is the case, there is the risk that he will not be thoroughly trained in his disciplines. This will produce increased frustrations as you attempt to control his behavior and keep him at his tasks.

Training junior to work with pup is an exercise in patience. Photo courtesy of Mike Baskerville.

Remember that there are no short cuts to dog training. Yard training is as critical for junior as it was for pup. There are some slight differences in the field-training routines because pup will be available to assist in a couple of areas. But yard training remains essentially the same (See chapters 4 and 5).

The only difference in junior's yard training is an emphasis on the privacy rule. Pup will undoubtedly be a source of distraction for junior and you will need all of your trainer's skills to keep him quiet. It's best to keep him in the pen while you work with junior. Junior is entitled to an opportunity to learn his exercises. There will be enough interference without pup getting into the act.

Cover all the basic commands and routines with Junior exactly as you did with pup. To place him in the field before he has thoroughly learned these basic exercises will do him a great disservice and increase your frustration level.

Field Training - The Methods

There are at least three basic methods at your disposal to field train junior. The first approach is simply to put junior down with pup and let him follow him wherever he goes. This method is based on your trust in pup's ability to teach junior all he needs to know, without picking up any bad habits or faults in the process.

The second method is to train him alone until he has learned his basic field exercises. When this is completed, junior can be placed with pup to hunt.

For repeated violations of discipline, leash both dogs if necessary.

The third method, which I prefer, is a combination of the other two approaches. Regardless of which method you chose, your training skills and judgment will be tested.

The first method involves a minimum of trainer involvement. Pup will, in fact, be teaching junior the art of rabbit hunting. This approach can work if these important criteria are met:

1. Junior is physically able to keep up with pup.
2. Pup is free from faults or bad habits that you don't want passed on to junior.
3. Pup is exceptional in all of his skills and abilities.

If junior is less than six months old, he will automatically be placed at a disadvantage when working with pup. After all, pup is capable of handling fences, ditches and other obstacles. If junior cannot keep up, he is likely to become discouraged very quickly. If pushed by the trainer to compete with the larger dog, he can become dispirited. He may or may not injure himself, but if he does he may become permanently flawed. This happens infrequently, but you will need to weigh the risk.

Does pup, now the lead dog, exhibit any faults that you don't want junior to learn? For example, does he habitually open on a cold line? Does he open frequently scent on game other than rabbits? Does he constantly attempt to hunt on his own, out of reasonable range? If he has a tendency toward these or other faults, it's a good bet that junior will soon be mirroring these mistakes. You will then be required to handle not just one but two problem dogs.

Is pup weak in any of his hunting abilities? Is he just a little lazy when it comes to working the thick stuff? Does he habitually push the rabbit too fast, resulting in frequent overrunning the line? Or is he too slow on the line, allowing the scent line to grow cold? If junior's training consists exclusively of running with pup, he will almost always learn the bad habits first.

Be assured that this method of putting junior with pup will work. Whether to use it is basically a judgment you will need to make. For many successful owners, putting the young pup with an older dog or even a pack of older dogs is the only system they have ever used, and they are convinced it's the only way to train.

The second method, working junior exclusively on his own, follows the exact routine you used previously to train pup. It requires keeping pup in the carrier box while you work junior alone, finding scent lines by kicking out rabbits, training junior to refrain from eating carrion, conditioning him to the gun, teaching him the command to check a certain area, getting him to respond to the here-he-is command, handling fence crossings, learning to hunt close as well as the other disciplines outlined in Chapters 7 and 8.

Finally, when he opens on a scent line, he can be placed with pup to work out his place as a team member. This method is ideal, providing you have sufficient time available to spend with him individually and still have sufficient time to allow pup his field work. Remember that pup is in the carrier box, so keep it secured and covered. The individual method is sometimes your only option if junior is less than six months old and/or small for his age.

The third method, the combination, works extremely well if junior is physically capable of following pup into the brush. If he is too small, you will need to split time between the dogs, allowing junior additional time to grow. Usually, six-month-old puppies possess the physical ability and stamina to follow the larger dog into the brush.

When you arrive at your training area, put both dogs down together. At first, the penmates will probably play, but don't be unduly alarmed at this behavior. Allow a few minutes of playtime, but be prepared to place limits on them. Junior doesn't understand anything about field work at this point and is just out for a good time. Use the no command as needed. If repeated violations of discipline occur, use the five-minute leash penalty for either or both dogs.

Once both dogs have settled down, get pup into the brush. Use the check command to accomplish this task. You want pup to learn to ignore junior and find that scent line as quickly as possible.

After pup has disappeared into the thick stuff, junior will wonder what's happening. He may follow pup immediately or he may remain close to you and whine. This is natural and should not be a cause of concern. Remember that this is all very new to junior and it will take time for him to figure it all out. Encourage him to follow pup, but don't insist. Be patient. When pup strikes a line and opens, let him work for several minutes. Keep an eye on junior. If he stays close by you or attempts to follow pup, that's fine. But if he begins to wander off on his own, ignoring either you or the race pup is running, quickly leash him and talk to him in soothing tones.

Now watch for the rabbit to either break into the clear or pass nearby through the vegetation. If junior is on a leash, quickly lead him to the exact spot where you last saw the rabbit. If junior is unleashed, call him to follow you to the line using the here-he-is command. Once on the line, unleash him (if leashed) and let him work the scent for as long as he wants. Be sure to praise him for these efforts.

When pup, who has been on the line, arrives, ignore him. Junior will be distracted at first, but keep encouraging him to stay with the line. Meanwhile, pup will most likely ignore junior and continue the race. If junior wants to follow along, that's perfectly okay. He probably won't go far before he returns to you. At this point, pour on the praise. Let him know you are pleased with him. This will build his confidence and fire his enthusiasm. Remember, he still wants to please you.

Repeat this routine as often as possible. Pup is being used to kick the rabbits out for you. The more rabbits he flushes, the more scent lines junior will get to work. This results in junior learning to follow scent lines. After many repetitions of this routine, he will open and tongue on the line.

After pup has flushed and run several rabbits, leash both dogs and return to your vehicle. Place pup in the carrier box, and weather permit-

You drop the tailgate and both dogs pile out together.

ting, cover the box with a canvas or tarp. This will help keep him quiet.
Now put junior down on his own and work with him exactly as you
worked pup during his exploratory trips. Junior needs to learn the
different scents, explore and respond to commands, refrain from eating
carrion, handle fences and other obstacles, hunt within a reasonable
range and work over the gun. As you train him individually, he will
become disciplined in these exercises and easier to manage.

Each time you run pup and junior together, you will need to watch
for problems so you can dispatch corrective measures immediately. An
example: While pup is working a line, junior may decide to go off on his
own and find his own scent line, ignoring you and pup. Correct this
quickly by leashing junior, keeping him with you until pup finishes his
race. If you fail to correct junior, he will assume he can take off any time
and any where to hunt on his own. This is contrary to your goal of
training both dogs to work as a team and work one scent line together.

Training junior to work with pup is an exercise in patience and is
often frustrating. But continue to be repetitious and persistent. Pup is
experienced enough by now to ignore junior's mistakes. But be aware of
pup's mistakes as well. If in your judgment, he is outside his disciplines,

don't hesitate to leash him. It's not unusual to have both dogs leashed at the same time because both have committed offenses. These penalties, however, are imposed less frequently as the dogs gain experience hunting as a team.

How long will it take to accomplish the goal of pup and junior hunting together? That depends on how much time you can spend working with them, your skills as a trainer and the personalities of the individual dogs. Usually, one or two seasons is sufficient, but it can vary.

Special Problems in the Field

The following two problems and corrections are not the only problems you will encounter as you strive to weld pup and junior into a well-meshed brace. But they will provide you with some guidance in handling a pair of stubborn, independent, temperamental hunting Beagles.

Line Jumping

It's a cool, clear morning with a light frost. There is no noticeable wind. The sky is clear and the autumn colors are ablaze. The sun has been up for only a few minutes when you arrive at your favorite running grounds. You quickly but quietly slip into your hunting boots, put on your safety vest, sling your possibles bag over your shoulder and stretch your legs as a hedge against muscle pulls and strains. Retrieving your gun (or walking staff), you turn your attention to the covered carrier box containing pup and junior. As you open the carrier box, both dogs show their excitement by wagging their tails and issuing low-frequency whines. They are eager to hit the ground running. You drop the truck's tailgate and both dogs pile out together.

The dogs sniff the ground excitedly and explore every inch for a hot scent line. You walk away from the truck at a slow pace. All the while, you are giving verbal encouragement to both dogs. They dart in and out of the thick cover, thrashing the weeds and brush, desperately searching for that hot line.

Suddenly, pup strikes a hot line. You know that it's pup because his tongue is distinctly different from junior's. Within seconds, junior joins the race, telling you and pup that he is part of the action. The rabbit makes his initial circle. It's a short loop, as he tries to evade the dogs. You wait until he breaks from the thick stuff. Momentarily, he darts out, but just as quickly, he disappears into the maze of weeds and thickets. Both dogs are giving full tongue as they show themselves in an opening, squarely on the line.

As they disappear into the thick stuff, pup stops tonguing while junior continues to turn up the volume. You wait patiently for pup to open. Endless minutes pass. Junior is tonguing steadily and working the line. Still nothing from pup. The race continues for several minutes when suddenly pup opens again. But he is nearly 100 yards ahead of junior.

Junior catches up with him shortly. Again, pup goes silent mouth (stops barking). The same thing happens again. This time you see pup flush the rabbit. Junior is still about 60 yards behind him. Pup opens and moves the rabbit toward you. You could easily bag it but let it pass. Your concern is pup's strange behavior. What's going on here?

This situation is known as jumping the line. It usually happens unexpectedly and most frequently among inexperienced penmates. However, it can also happen among more experienced penmates. It is a frustrating experience and there are no guaranteed preventive actions.

Why does it happen? One theory holds that because both dogs are competitive, one is attempting to show the other he can move the rabbit without help. Another theory is that the offending dog, pup in this case, is jealous of junior and is determined to show he is Number One Dog. Whichever theory is true, what's important is knowing how to minimize the problem.

If the line-jumping dog commits the offense only occasionally, it's probably best to ignore it. However, if this behavior becomes habitual, you will need to take corrective action. One solution is to leash the offender for five to 10 minutes, allowing the other dog to hunt alone during the penalty time. After the penalty time expires and pup is returned to the hunt, allow him to hunt as long as he doesn't commit the offense again. If he does it again, leash him again. This time, keep him on the leash until junior has opened on another rabbit. Pup is going to be very unhappy with this arrangement, as will be evidenced by his howling and whining. But this action will certainly get his attention. If he is not going to hunt with his partner, he will just have to miss out on the hunt.

A note of caution is needed here. Use this technique sparingly. If you overuse it, you might find that the non-offending dog will refuse to hunt without the other one. If the line-jumping problem becomes habitual, try running each dog alone for a few sessions. Usually, Beagles will learn to hunt together without you resorting to these drastic measures.

The Split Race

It's another bluebird morning. The air is cool, crisp and clear. There is no wind. The sun is beginning to appear beyond the eastern horizon.

The topsoil is frozen but there is no frost. You have selected a new area to run after getting permission from the land owner, who told you the rabbits are so plentiful they are becoming a nuisance.

Both dogs are in a honeysuckle thicket, tunneling through the maze of greenery. Suddenly, junior strikes a hot line. You see the rabbit flush 40 yards to your left. Junior is giving full cry, madly trying to keep on the line. You wait, expecting pup to honor junior's strike and join the race. After an anxious minute, pup strikes but he is headed off to the right. You see the second rabbit flush and hear pup tonguing at the top of his voice. Meanwhile, junior is going out of hearing range on his own line to your left.

This situation is commonly referred to as "split lines" or "split races." It is a problem that can try a trainer's patience. When it happens in familiar areas, it is not overly difficult to solve. But when running unfamiliar areas, it raises the blood pressure and increases anxiety because the trainer is not familiar with the regular rabbit runs.

There are two basic options available to the trainer. Both require judgment and awareness.

The first option is to allow each dog to run his individual race, trusting each will circle the rabbit completely back to its starting point. This requires that the owner know the personalities and abilities of each dog thoroughly. If one dog still lacks the ability to hold a line consistently, this option is suspect. It is further complicated if the trainer is unfamiliar with the hunting grounds. Are there roads or residences nearby? Are there trap lines or other hazards that could endanger a dog concentrating on a line?

The second option, while more difficult to accomplish, is usually the best. It requires judgment as well as quick action. Pup struck the second line and is closer to you. Go to him immediately and place him on the leash. Do not scold or discipline him in any way. It makes little sense to discipline him for doing what he was trained to do. When you have him leashed, listen for junior. If he is in a long check, you will have some anxious moments waiting to hear him open again. If he doesn't open after several minutes, take pup with you on the leash and return to the place where junior first struck the line. Be sure to keep pup leashed the entire time. If you still cannot hear junior, begin walking toward the point where you last saw him and/or the rabbit, stopping frequently to listen. Don't let pup off his leash, even if you happen to kick up another rabbit. When you locate junior either by sight or sound, go to him immediately and place him on a leash also. Again, don't punish or scold.

When both dogs are leashed, return to the area where the dogs struck their individual hot lines and begin your run again. While there is no guarantee, there's a good chance both dogs will now work together.

The split-line problem occurs most frequently when both dogs are beginning to learn to work as a team. However, it occurs occasionally among more experiences braces. It's important that you resolve it quickly when it occurs. If it becomes a continuos problem, you will need to determine which dog is the primary offender. The offender is the dog who strikes and opens second, refusing to honor the one who struck and opened first. Use the five-minute leash penalty to correct it.

There can be other aggravations and frustrations resulting from working more that one dog, such as running unwanted game (especially deer), or responding to unknown packs. But these minor inconveniences are a part of the sport. They are challenges that will try your skill and patience. Just consider them payment of dues to the sport of training and working the rabbit-hunting beagle.

Bill Bennett with his brace of Beagles, Sadie (L) and Ben.

Bibliography

Beagle, Marvia Foy & Anna K. Nichols, TFH Publications, Inc., Ltd., 1985.

Beagles, Lucia Vriends-Parent, Barrons Educational Series, Inc., 1987.

Caring For Your Puppy, John L. Mara, DVM, Hills Pet Products, Topeka, Ks., 1989.

Complete Book of the Dog, The,Angela Sayer, Multimedia Books, Limited, 1989.

Complete Dog Book, The, AKC Inc., Humell Book House, MacMillian Publishing Inc., 1985.

Feeding For Breeding, Alpo Pet Center, Allentown, Pa. 1989.

Guide to Vaccinating Your Dog, Norden Laboratories, USA, 1990.

Hunting Dogs of America, The, Jeff Griffen, Doubleday & Company, Garden City NY.

Outdoor Life, 2 Park Ave, New York, N.Y., Sept. 1989.

Prescription Diet, Hills Pet Products, Topeka, Ks., 1989.

Ultimate Dog Book, The, David Taylor, Simon & Shuster, 1990.

United States Bureau of the Census, United States Government Printing Office, Washington, D.C.

Appendix

Where to Locate Beagles: Breeders, Kennels, Information

The American Kennel Club
51 Madison Avenue
New York NY 10010

The American Rabbit Hound Association
PO Box 244
Hoskinston KY 40844
606/374-5938

Beagle Adoption Service
Bill and Janel Nielan
7092 Kermore Lane
Stanton GA 90680

The National Beagle Club
Joseph B. Wiley Jr.
River Road
Bedminster NJ 07921

The American Rabbit Hound Association (ARHA) Kennels

Abby Road Kennels
Bob Kirby
3230 Altoaloma Dr
Birmingham AL 35216
205/822-5558

Adams Red River Kennels
Floyd H Adams
PO Box 574
Dover TN 37058
615/827-2199

Anderson's Big Creek Kennel
Mike & Dee Anderson
Rt 4 Box 87
Jonesboro AR 72401
501/932-6386

Appalachian M Kennel
Everett Morgan
PO Box 244
Hoskinston KY 40844
606/374-5938

B & R Kennel
Pete Baker & Jesse Rogers
377 Kilarney Dr
Winchester KY 40391
606/374-1668

Barkeyville Beagles
Glenn C Adams
Rd 1 Box 346
Harrisville PA 16038-9645
814/786-7821

Bell's Run Kennels
Bill Damiano
Rd #2 Box 77
Tyrone PA 16686
814/742-8522

Ben's Beagle Barn
Ben Snider
Rt 1 Box 36
Lapwai ID 83540
208/843-7158

Billoucliff Kennels
Clifford D Jenkins
2 Taylor Rd
Enfield CT 06082
203/749-4874

Chris' Kennel
Lloyd T Hern, Lloyd C Hearn &
Christopher Hearn
714 Belleau Dr
O'Fallon MO 63366
314/272-2471; 528-6212

Conway's Sangamo Kennel
Marshall & Nancy Conway
RR 7 Box 402
Decatur IL 62521
217/877-5994

Cook's Hilltop Kennels
Ron Cook
Rt 6 Box 100A
Murray KY 42971
502/436-2194

Cox's Sipsey Creek Kennel
Eddy & Seth Cox
Rt 4 Box 455
Hamilton AL 35570
205/921-9970

Crackerjack Basset Hounds & Wild
Rabbit Farm
Jack H Wells
Rt 1 Box 519
Huntsville TX 77340

Crooked Fork Kennels
Donnie & Rod Mullins, Greg Whitt
PO Box 80
McVeigh KY 41546
606/353-0535

Cypress Bayou Kennels
Ponchatoula LA
504/294-5393

Dogwood Kennels
Billy Fielder, Jimmy Winton
374 Riggs Ln
Tullahoma TN 37388
615/393-4699; 649-2031

Double Crowe Kennels
186 Double Rd
Renfrew PA 16053
Terry Crowe: 412/789-7459
Richard Double: 412/285-5007

Down East Beagle Kennel
Ray Dail
8400 Main St
PO Box 717
Vanceboro NC 28586
919/244-2480

Dry Bayou Beagles
John Jaggers, Jimmy Sullivan,
Chris Selby
PO Box 454
Portland AR 71663
John: 501/737-2730
Jimmy: 501/853-8082
Chris: 501/367-3656

Eastview Kennels
Quality Warfield Reds
Don McCutchen
PO Box 126
Monticello KY 42633
Days: 606/348-9327
Nights: 606/348-7060

Frontier Beagles
Roger Boggs, Harold Turner,
Freddy Day
HC 65 Box 320
Smilax KY 41764
606/279-4396; 279-4749

Gonella's Hickory Hills Beagles
Eastern-bred Crain Hounds
Michael Gonnella
PO Box 285
Fanwood NJ 07023
Day: 908/654-5785
Night: 908/232-8156

Green River Kennel
Oneal Basham
5840 Reedyville Rd
RoundHill KY 42275
502/286-4877

Guest Creek Kennels
Charles Franklin
6124 Zaringmill Rd
Shelbyville KY 40065
502/834-7653

Hale's Kennel
AKC & ARHA Blue Cap, Yellow
Creek & Pearson Creek
Graysville OH
614/934-2167

Hall's Knob Creek Kennels
"Hall's ARHA Dual Champion
Gun Dogs"
Chuck and Josh Hall
221 S. St. Gregory Rd
Rooster Run KY 40013
502/349-1957

Hall's Champion Gundogs
Terry Scharfenberger, Breeder/
Buyer
606/635-9569

Hall's Champion Gun Dogs
Scott Stallings, Breeder/Buyer
502/348/2568

Hi-Brass Beagles
Billy Clark
2040 Piney Grove Rd
Loganville GA 30249
404/466-8906

Hillside Gay Bred Beagle Kennel
Gary & Kathy Hawkins
11957 15 Mile Rd
Sterling Heights MI 48312
810/268-3458

Holliday Creek Beagles
Darrel Holliday
HC 68 Box 181
White Oak KY 41474
606/743-4042

JC's Dangerous Beagles
Jim Cockerham
15396 E 2000 S. Rd
Homence IL 60954
815/944-5000

Jackson's Mountain Kennel
Cecil Jackson
127 Wyn-Way
Boone NC 28607
704/264-6578

Jag's Kennels
Al & June Graham
Rt 1 Box 335-A
Lynchburg SC 29080
803/453-5451

KC's Riverside Kennels
Keith Cutshaw
Rt 1 Box 38C
Afton TN 37616
615/630-7225

Kane's Creek Beagles
Kenneth L. Moran
PO Box 160
Kingwood WV 26537
304/329-3000

Kellum Creek Kennel
Bryan & Wanda Ogle
1405 Douglas Dam Rd
Sevierville TN 37876
615/428-1885

Klaiber's Kennels
Grand Champion Klaiber's Bill
Mike & Jeremy Klaiber
PO Box 766
Ironton OH 45638-0766
614/532-9653

LFJ Kennel
Larry & Jerry Ifft, Fred Arnaut
2221 E Arms Dr
Hubbard OH 44425
216/759-8774

Lane's J & J Beagles
Jim Lane
Rt 81 Box 2
Peterstown WV 24963
304/753-5149

Linemaster Kennel
AKC & ARHA Gun Dogs
M L , M D & Joseph R Huff
117 Private Rd
11129 State Rte 243
South Point OH 45680
614/867-4818

Little D's Kennel
Tim & Debbi Rogers
Rt 7 Box 182M
Malvern AR 72104
501/332-2814

Lone Oak Kennels
Roger L Echelberry
2030 Fattler Ridge Rd
Philo OH 43711

MBL's Rice Capital Kennels
Monte B Lanier
522 S Ave G
Crowley LA 70526
318/788-3802

MJB's Spooky Bayou Kennels
Michael J Broussard
608 South Ave M
Crowley LA 70526
318/783-7724

Mac's Kennel
Brice McGlamery
1781 Hopewell Rd
Morganton NC 28655
704/433-8296

Marple's Red Hounds Kennel
Matthew Marple
7243 Elkhorn Rd
Knifley KY 42753
502/789-1804

Meramec Valley Beagles
Tim & Patty Hale
7274 Four Mile Rd
Washington MO 63090
314/239-5406

Missouri Ridge Kennels
Roger Johnson & Robert F
Johnson Jr.
Rt 1 Box 590
Cadet MO 63630
Roger: 314/586-4515
Robert: 314/438-6166

Missouri Rocky Hills Beagle
Kennel
Jon Stuart
Rt 1 Box 705
West Plains MO 65775
417/257-7726

Morning Star Kennel
Randy Thompson
Rt 2 Box 274-B
Bentonville AR 72712
501/273-0699

Mose's Fork MTN Kennel
Thomas & Betty Porter
Rt 1 Box 302
Dunlow WV 25511
304/385-4675

Murphy's Music Bottom Kennel
Ed Murphy
Rt 2 Box 287
Delbarton WV 25670
304/426-6260

Meyers, W L Kennel
Bill Meyers
1258 Reid Ave
Xenia OH 45685
513/372-2681

Nighthawk Kennels
Jr. Cooper, Ken Eaton, Charles Cole
1603 Daisy Dr
Rogers AR 72756
501/659-0967; 417/662-3721

O'B's Buffin Beagles
Mickey O'Bryan
1842 Doc Lindsey Rd
Fort Meade FL 33841
813/285-8542

Ohio River Kennel
Mark & Rob Blake
29 Meadow Ct
Wheelersburg OH 45694
614/574-8886

Owl Creek Kennel
Robt C Held Jr.
Alexandria KY 41001
606/635-9407

Penny Hill Kennel
David Smith & Sons
RR 2 Box 197
Murray KY 42071
502/759-9742

Pepper's Black Diamond Kennels
Mark Pepper
PO Box 364
Gideon MO 63848
314/448-3155

Pigeon Creek's Rabbit Run Kennel
Tim & Susan Seaton
Rt 1, 5045 Newport Hwy
Greenville TN 37743
615/638-9536

Plymal's Stagger Fork Kennels
Miles Plymal
Box 105
Hardy KY 41531
606/353-0258

Prewitt Bend Beagles
Denny & Connie Roberts
194 N Skyline Dr
Louisville KY 40229
502/955-8267

RAB's Kennel
Richard A Burel & Son
4052 Donna Ln SW
Loganville GA 30249
404/466-4928

RBN Beagles
Rowdy, Ben & Nick Holstine
1442 Hwy 83 S
Hartford WI 53027
414/673-0730

Red Hills Kennels
Ray Davis & Mike Rinehart
110 N Walnut, Box 100
Toluca IL 61369
815/452-2698; 452-2926

Ridge Runner Beagles
Daniel & J P Ward
412 Flucom Meadows
DeSoto MO 63020
314/337-2807

Ridge Runner Beagles II
Richard "Chuck" Dewey
PO Box 268
Fredericktown MO 63645
314/783-6137

Rising Sun Kennels
Paul B & Karl J Webb
1729 Lamberton
Middletown OH 45044
513/423-4578

Rocky Fork Beagles
AKC- & ARHA-Registered
Stewart Hungate & Jack Wallis Jr.
RR 1 Box 79
Roadhouse IL 62082
217/9274303; 374-6102

Rocky Ridge Kennel
Daniel Wolfe & Bill Lawless
28501 TR 205
Fresno OH 43824
614/545-9741

Roderick's Beagle & Basset Place
ARHA- & AKC-Registered
29566 60th Ave
Lawton MI 49065
616/624-6559

Rymanda's Kennel
Ryan & Deanna Thomas
314 Chicago Ave
Goshen IN 46526
219/534-1970

Saint's Melodious Beagle Kennel
Geo St Germain Jr & Tom Hess Sr
Rt 111, PO Box 77
Chesterfield IL 62830
618/753-3128

Salamonie River Kennels
AKC- & ARHA-Registered
Rex & Millie Bear
3984 W 8005
Warren IN 46792
219/468-4236

Sangamon Ridge Kennels
RR 1, Box 161
Monticello IL 62856
Randy Eades: 217/762-9698
Mike Eades: 217/762-9584
Fred Hausmann: 217/523-4190
Ron Eades: 217/762-7215

Sandy Run Kennel
Virgil Church, Keith Lloyd
820 South Post Rd
Shelby NC 28152
704/482-8236; 434-5453

Seymour's Hickory Hill's Beagles
Oddie Seymour
685 Western Park
Memphis TN 38109
901/785-0531

Shady Creek Kennels
Phillip Richie, Jamie Hilbert
144 Higdon Loop
New Haven KY 40051
502/348-0704; 549-7616

Shoal Creek Kennels
Randle Jones, Don Bennett
La Grange GA 30241
706/882-2606

Sill's 5/8 Kennel
Gale & Shirley Sill
PO Box 93
Kinmundy IL 62854
618/547-7716

Smith's Kennels
R Gene Smith, Gary Palmer
86 W Clarksville Rd
Clarksville OH 45113
513/289-2163

Smokey Mountain Kennels
Roger Parrot
106 Browning Branch Rd
Waynesville NC 28786
704/452-9232

Snake Kennel
Fred Bach, Tom Langenhorst
5822 Billhortz Rd
New Baden IL 62265
Days: 618/234-9793
Nights: 618/588-4902

Spiders Gray Rock
Tommy Oliver
755 South Maple St
Lebanon TN 37087
615/443-3471

Stump Town Kennel
Lloyd J Conn
201 West Center
Leroy IL 61752
309/962-6121

Stump's Ky MTN Kennel
Mark Stump
4752 Upper Johns Creek Rd
Kimper KY 41539
Business: 606/835-4447
Home: 606/835-2636

Sugar Mountain Kennel
8015 Thompson-Sharpsville Rd
Masury OH 44438
Jeff & Mary Laney: 216/448-4179
Chuck & Judy Laney:896-4964

Sundance Kennels
Carl Pease
Box 277 Rt1
Francisco IN 47469
812/782-3260

Swartz Powerhouse Kennel
Mark A Swartz
218 Eaton Rd
Winchester KY 40391
606/744-3812

Talk That Talk Kennel
Larry Ramey
1358 Valley Road
Owingsville KY 40360

Tarheel Kennel
Royce & Shannon Farlow
5479 Zoo Parkway
Asheboro NC 27203
910/629-5866

Timber Time Kennels
Michael Boyd
PO Box 989
Vansant VA 24656
703/597-2438

Top Gun Beagles
Joe Morgan
3541 Willow Wind Ct
Loganville GA 30249
404/466-6767

Tracko
Ronald McCalla
553 Hagenbuch St
Urbana OH 43078
513/653-4627

Triple "A" Kennel
Douglas M Arnette Jr.
PO Box 179
Windsor VA 23487
804/357-0008

Twin-A-Beagles
Juan Armitage & family
Olympia KY 40358
606/768-6425

Two Mile Creek Kennel
RR 1 Box 268
Sullivan IL 61951
217-728-7630

Walker's Bluegrass Beagles
Rick Walker
310 N 6th St
Hamilton OH 45011
513/856-9860

Wehmeyer Badgerland Beagles
Roger Weymeyer
721 Johnson St
Beloit WI 53511
608/364-4435

Wild Woods Kennel
Kevin Bowling
30 Bailey Rd
London KY 40741
606/843-7738

Wildcat Combine
Kenny Vanhoose, Kenny Webb,
Sam Lebeau
2210 Sanders Rd
Ashland KY 41101
606/325-1174

Wildwest Kennels
Ron West
RR 3 Box 95
Palmyra IL 62674
217/484-6494

Woodland Kennel
Rick & Trudy Hunt
Rt 5 Box 90A
Sedalia MO 65301
816/827-2006

Index